The True Power of Water

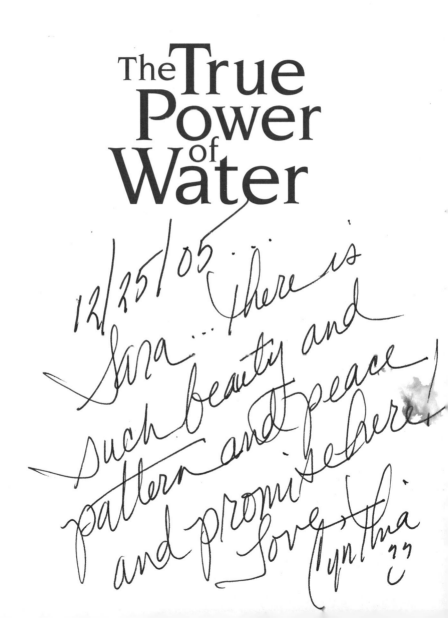

12/25/05 ... there is
Sara ...
such beauty and
pattern and peace
and promise here!
love, Cynthia

Sara D. Brunillo, Ph.D.

The True Power of Water

HEALING AND DISCOVERING OURSELVES

Masaru Emoto

Translated by
Noriko Hosoyamada

BEYOND
WORDS
Publishing
I N C

Beyond Words Publishing, Inc.
20827 N.W. Cornell Road, Suite 500
Hillsboro, Oregon 97124-9808
503-531-8700

Managing editors: Sarabeth Blakey and Julie Steigerwaldt
Copyeditor/Proofreader: Marvin Moore
Design: Jerry Soga
Composition: William H. Brunson Typography Services

Printed in Korea

Distributed to the book trade by Publishers Group West

Library of Congress Cataloging-in-Publication Data

Emoto, Masaru, 1943–
    [Mizu no maryoku. English]
    The true power of water / Masaru Emoto ; translated by
Noriko Hosoyamada.
        p. cm.
    ISBN 1-58270-128-8
    1. Water—Health aspects.   2. Water—Philosophy.
    I. Title.

RA591.5.E45813   2005
613.2'87—dc22

2005000691

The corporate mission of Beyond Words Publishing, Inc.:
Inspire to Integrity

T A B L E   O F   C O N T E N T S

Although I have studied water for a long time, my educational training was not originally in science. At Yokohama City University, I majored in American-Chinese Relations at the Department of International Relations, the Faculty of Humanities and Sciences. My background is in liberal arts. It wasn't until 1987, at age forty-three, when I encountered the wonder and mystery of water. I was working in the trading business at the time, and one of my counterparts introduced me to a type of water that worked miraculously on my foot pain. This experience fascinated me.

My fascination led me to study water deeply, and over time I became convinced that water took in information. I do not mean the information we receive when we watch television or listen to news on the radio or read articles in magazines and newspapers. Instead, I'm referring to the external factors that affect the mind and body. For example, when you look at beautiful scenery, you feel peaceful. When you listen to beautiful music, you feel your heart purified. I use *information* to mean all of these external factors that affect our mind and body.

I have come to the conclusion through my many years of research that water changes its quality according to the information it takes in. Unfortunately, this rather radical idea, which upsets the common sense of conventional science, was not well received. I needed to find something that could be used as physical evidence for this idea.

One day, I casually opened a book, *The Day That Lightning Chased the Housewife: And Other Mysteries of Science*, by David Savold and Julia Leigh (editor), and one heading caught my eye: "Are there any identical snow crystals?"

This book made the point that no two crystals of snow, over millions of years, have ever been identical. As a child, I had learned this. It wasn't anything new. However, in the context of my search, I was thrilled by this line, which was nothing more than mere common sense.

A new idea flashed in my mind: What if I freeze water and look at its crystals? Immediately, I told a young researcher to begin an experiment. (The details of the experiment will be explained later in the book.) After two months of struggle, he was able, in September 1994, to take a picture of a beautiful hexagonal frozen ice crystal. It was the first water-crystal picture ever taken.

Naturally, when I first published my discoveries about water in a book titled *Hado no Shinri* (The truth of wave fluctuation) (PHP Publishing, November 1994), I had no idea that my work would be received with surprise and appreciation from the world and would resonate so strongly with people. I supposed that somebody else must have thought of a similar thing and perhaps used it for a long time.

Since then, I have been hooked by water. After we succeeded in photographing water crystals in 1994, we accumulated water-crystal pictures for the next five years. During this time, I published some books on the subject of *hado* (the energy or vibration inherent in all things, which will be explained in more detail later) and my water research, and I presented my work at three academic meetings. However, I met no one who knew about similar studies.

In late 1998, I presented my work at the meeting of the Society for Human Body Science held at Tenri University. Dr. Kazuo Murakami, a well-known gene researcher and professor at Tukuba University (currently professor emeritus), happened to be in the audience. His compliment was the first that I had ever received from a scientist of authority.

Consequently, I made the decision to publish my photos in a book titled *Messages from Water*, published by my wife, Kazuko. The time of publication was set for June 1999, and I ventured to add an English translation to the whole text and to begin the subtitle with the word *Sekaihatsu* (World first). Using both Japanese and English for the explanations of each picture in the book changed my life, as many foreigners paid attention to it. The book has now been translated into twenty-three languages.

Time has flown, and it has been six years since then. Now I receive invitations to speak on the topics of water and *hado* from all over the world.

The interest in and response to the material I present has been overwhelming. About three years ago I was interviewed by the public-relations director at Siemens. After the interview I heard that the company had started to provide hado water (water given good energy) at its cafeteria. In Augsburg, I am invited every year to speak to approximately one thousand people about hado. Since 2002, they have used Hado for the name of their symposium. *Hado* has become an independent word in Germany.

In the Netherlands, I had the honor to meet with Princess Irene, a sister of Queen Beatrix. Princess Irene is a naturalist, and she invited seven or eight scholars to individual discussions. I was chosen to be a representative intellectual regarding water. These discussions, including one with the famous British biologist Rupert Sheldrake, were published in Dutch. (Please see the back of this book for more details on available books.)

In North America, I have lectured in a number of cities in the United States and twice at Harvard University, and I have received many speaking requests from Canada, where there is a high interest in nature and environmental problems. During my seminar tour of Canada in May 2003, I visited Victoria, Vancouver, Calgary, Edmonton, Montreal, and Toronto, where SARS (severe acute respiratory syndrome) was a major subject of attention.

The more countries I visit, the more people I resonate with. However, I have yet to meet an individual who is doing similar work or who knows about someone doing it. An ordinary man like me with no exceptional knowledge or connection to natural science and religion has become a water researcher lecturing throughout the world and writing books on water, one after another, for publication and translation. This fact shows how little research on water has been conducted elsewhere and how long the true power of water has been neglected.

An adult body is 70 percent water. Therefore, in terms of materials, we can say that we are water. Yet, water has hardly been investigated up until now. Perhaps that is why we don't understand other people, nor do we understand the essence of ourselves.

Usually, we drink water without paying much attention to it. We know that water is important to maintain our life, but because of its familiarity, very rarely do we consciously appreciate it. Here are a few questions and ideas to ponder, questions that we'll explore in this book:

- How seriously do you think about the characteristics of water?
- Are you aware that the water you drink has the ability to improve your health and your life?
- Do you know that your consciousness has the ability to change water? When you send your gratitude to water, its quality improves. When you call water by names or ignore it, it deteriorates.

The twenty-first century is said to be the Age of Aquarius, and in astrology, Aquarius is the sign of the water bearer. And the United Nations has designated the year 2005 as "The Beginning of the Decade of Water (2005–2014)." We must not make this just fanfare.

Let's learn about water more and more. Let's pay attention to water more and more. Then let's learn more about ourselves. The more you know about water, the more clearly you will see yourself. As you become clearer, you will see the society, the nation, the world, the earth, the universe, and eventually the divine being. It is because "Water is the first principle of all things," as the Greek philosopher Thales said.

If this book provides you with an opportunity to have a positive thought about water and to think about what it means to live healthily and happily, it is the greatest pleasure for me as the author.

I am indebted to Kodansha's Mr. Akihiro Maruki, chief of the life culture department, and Ms. Azusa Shinmi, editor, for the publication of this book in Japan. Thanks also to Noriko Hosoyamada for her translation into English and to Beyond Words Publishing for publishing it in English. On behalf of water, I express my gratitude. Finally, to all readers, I offer my love and gratitude.

~~~~~~~~~~~~

CHAPTER ONE

The Process of Discovery

How the Research Began

As I mentioned in the introduction, I came up with the idea of photographing water crystals when I casually opened a book and saw the heading "Are there any identical snow crystals?"

Fortunately, my trading company employed Mr. Kazuya Ishibashi, a researcher who had studied applied sciences as his doctorate program at Kumamoto University. Naturally, he was skilled in observing things through microscopes. I leased a high-precision microscope and instructed him to take a picture of ice crystals. Mr. Ishibashi looked at me questioningly, and I told him emphatically, "I am sure of it. We should be able to take water-crystal pictures, absolutely."

This young man was not so sure. With a serious look, he said, "Mr. Emoto, my knowledge and experience tells me that we will not succeed in taking pictures of water crystals."

I said, "It can be done. You seem doubtful, but I am confident of this. Trust me and please try hard, and you will be able to take photos of water crystals."

For two months after I gave him the order, he repeated the work of freezing water and looking at it through the microscope. Day in and day out, he would examine ice through the microscope, only to be disappointed. Meanwhile, I would wait for him to finish his work late at night and take him out for a drink. Fortunately, he was fond of drinking sake then. Drinking his favorite sake would cheer him up even when he came up short in achieving the results in the laboratory.

The only thing that I, who didn't have the skills for doing the experiment, could do was make an appeal and comfort him. I tried to motivate Mr. Ishibashi so that he would continue to try hard in the laboratory.

My wife often says that it is fortunate that Mr. Ishibashi did the work and not me, considering his efforts. I agree that the reason we could succeed in taking a crystal picture for the first time in the world was because I left the work with Mr. Ishibashi, who had perseverance. After two months of hard work, we managed to take one water-crystal picture at last.

I will never forget Mr. Ishibashi's face when he dashed out of the laboratory holding the picture to show me. Thinking about our attitude at that time, I realize that both his and my intention was pure for the challenging task of taking water-crystal pictures. Mr. Ishibashi, who was initially doubtful, must have been eventually influenced by my passion because he became confident about the work we were doing. That is why water must have shown its beautiful shape to us. If our intention had been to make money, I don't think water would have responded to our grasping spirit and formed crystals.

As we continued to conduct our experiments and take pictures, we gathered a better understanding of how best to conduct the experiments. Later, we installed three large freezers that could maintain the temperature at a constant $-5\,^{\circ}$C ($23\,^{\circ}$F).

How do we take our pictures? Let me introduce you to our current methods. First, we put a water sample in a glass bottle and expose it to information, such as a word, picture, or music, for some time. Then, this water is dropped on fifty petri dishes (5 cm, or 2.5 inches in diameter). These dishes are then frozen in a freezer at −25°C (−13°F) or lower. When they are taken out three hours later, ice grains have been formed with their center rolled up due to surface tension. These grains are very small (less than one-half inch). We then direct light on each grain of ice and look at it through the microscope.

If things go well, a crystal starts to form as the temperature rises and the ice starts to melt. Taking one to two minutes, it opens up like a blooming flower. The fifty petri dishes contain the same water frozen at the same condition. However, not all ice grains form crystals. While the ice in some dishes forms beautiful crystals, ice in other dishes doesn't show any crystals at all. (See figure 1.1.)

When we take statistics, we can categorize the results in groups, such as those that have many obviously similar beautiful crystals, those that tend to have many collapsed crystals, and those that have no crystals. Therefore, water crystals are certainly indicative of the quality of water we studied.

The State of Our Water: Natural, Tap, and Mineral
As we continued photographing water, I noticed something. Tap water didn't form crystals at all, while natural, untreated water—not exactly recognized for its quality—did. The beauty of these water crystals was intriguing; the "tentacles" were stretching out-

ward freely and easily from the hexagonal base. On the other hand, I couldn't believe my eyes when I saw pictures of frozen tap water. Quite honestly, I viewed their grotesque forms with loathing. Far from crystal formation, the ice often showed horrible shapes.

This got me thinking about how more and more people are dissatisfied with tap water, especially in developed countries where chlorine is added to disinfect it. Such treated water is neither tasty nor good for health, so people seek safe water in the form of mineral water, even if they have to pay a higher price for it. I decided to research the crystal formation of natural water, tap water, and mineral water to compare the quality.

Often people say that I need to define what I mean by "natural water." If we were to define it as the water that is yet to have a human influence, there would be no "natural water" on earth. We humans have definitely contaminated the air. In our atmosphere, water forms clouds and falls back onto the earth as rain. After the rain hits the surface of the ground, it seeps into the earth, which we have also contaminated. So, water cannot be said to have no human influence.

I do not intend to demand such a strict attitude to define "natural water." As I see it, "natural water" is the water sprung from the earth after the rainfall has been filtered through Mother Earth.

Our testing of natural and tap water revealed interesting findings. The tap water at my office in Tokyo didn't form crystals. On the other hand, natural water showed crystals. Overall, the tap water in Tokyo was not good. We took pictures of the tap water sampled at various spots in Tokyo, but none yielded a crystal.

We then sampled and photographed tap water from other cities: to the north, Hokkaido; to the south, Kyushu and Okinawa. Cities such as Sapporo, Sendai, Nagoya, Kanazawa, Osaka, Hiroshima, Fukuoka, and Naha didn't have the tap water that could form a shape worthy to be called crystal. Interestingly, the tap water in Katano City, in northern Osaka near the borders of the prefectures of Kyoto and Nara, produced beautiful crystals, as it included 60 percent groundwater.

I expected good water in Asia, but I found that the water was no good in Hong Kong, Macao, and Bangkok.

How about the water in Europe? Every time I visited big cities in Europe such as London, Paris, and Rome, I sampled and took pictures of the tap water, but the frozen water formed shapes far from crystals. The tap water in Venice, which has been regarded as the capital of water, was a little better than that of the other cities, but it also formed shapes far from crystals.

The cities that didn't disappoint us for their tap water were Vancouver, Canada; Buenos Aires, Argentina; and Manaus, Brazil. I was impressed by their water, which formed beautiful crystals, unlike the tap water in other places. All of these cities are located near a natural water source. It has been years since we did the work, so I don't know if these cities' tap water is still capable of forming crystals, but I am hopeful that it is. (See figure 1.2.)

Collecting samples of spring water all over Japan was indeed exciting. Eighty percent of Japan is mountainous. As Japan is situated in the wet temperate zone of Asia, we have lots of rain, which is absorbed by mountains and forests. After it is filtered through the ground, the water springs in many locations in Japan. No other developed nations are as rich as Japan in terms of natural water.

Water that goes through this natural filtration system is tasty and good for our health. So Japan is now in the midst of an unprecedented natural-water boom. Someone did an interesting comparison: The price of water is about the same as that of oil, although the price of oil includes a huge amount for the contract, shipping, and refining. Depending on the type, water can be more expensive than oil.

One thing is for certain: Many people who want to drink good natural water are willing to pay a high price.

However, even expensive natural water is beginning to be polluted. According to a test conducted by the Hygiene Institute of Yokohama City, chemical substances are detected in some mineral waters. Their findings were reported on the first page of the newspaper *Mainichi* on April 20, 2003. The article states as follows:

It was revealed that the Hygiene Institute of Yokohama City detected the chemical substances formaldehyde and acetaldehyde in some mineral water sold in Japan. Compared to the measurements of the city's tap water, some products contained more than 80 times as much. However, the amount is not considered harmful to human health. The quality of mineral water is regulated according to the standards under the Food Hygiene Act; the number of criteria is fewer than those for tap water. Japan's Ministry of Health, Labor, and Welfare launched the task to establish new water standards for mineral water in the fall of last year. However, they are undecided as to how to handle the aldehydes.

The survey was conducted on the bottled mineral water sold in Yokohama City. Among the thirty items surveyed, fourteen of them were imported from America, France, and

Canada, and sixteen were domestic water samples drawn from ten prefectures. Using the analysis method developed by the institute, the water was examined for formaldehyde and acetaldehyde.

As a result, the aldehydes were detected in the water of nineteen items—five imported and fourteen domestic. Among the nineteen items, seventeen contained both formaldehyde and acetaldehyde.

The highest concentration of formaldehyde found was in one of the domestic waters, with 59 grams per liter. For acetaldehyde, one of the waters from America measured 260 grams per liter. Both surpassed the measurements of Yokohama City's tap water (13 micrograms of formaldehyde and 3.1 micrograms of acetaldehyde).

In Japan, mineral water is classified as a soft drink and has to meet the standard specifications set under the Food Hygiene Act, which does not have specifications for aldehydes. On the other hand, the water-purity standards for tap water include formaldehyde as a control item, and its indicator value (with monitoring for not exceeding this value) is set for 80 micrograms per liter.

The causes for these impure substances are thought to be either at the source or during the manufacturing process, but the institute commented, "It's not clear." No relation to the materials of the containers was confirmed.

Epidemiological studies have verified formaldehyde as a carcinogen. It is considered as the causal substance for sick-house syndrome and chemical hypersensitivity. Acetaldehyde is confirmed as a carcinogen in animal tests.

What I feared has become a reality: mineral water contaminated by human hands. Not many people are aware of this in Japan; however, it has been discussed as a probable situation for a while in the West.

Next we decided to take pictures of mineral-water crystals. Among the three brands we selected, two domestic ones formed beautiful crystals. I hope that this wasn't an accident and that the water will stay good. (See figure 1.3.)

In the future, quite a few mineral-water companies will be forced into a tight corner, because in the West people have already started to stay away from mineral water.

When I visited Canada for my speaking engagement, I bought a very interesting water. It was remineralized water sold by a well-known company.

The word *remineralized* indicates that the minerals originally contained in the water are taken out and then some minerals necessary for humans are added back to the water.

Ample minerals get into water during the process of filtration through the earth. So far, we have been appreciative of these minerals and take them into our body. Interestingly, the popular product I encountered was capitalizing on the fact that these minerals had been taken out.

In this case, it would be more accurate to call it "distilled water" rather than "natural water." When I went to Canada one year earlier, I hadn't noticed it. But this time I saw it everywhere. I recall that when I flew Air Canada, the water was also served in-flight.

This is the current situation of "natural water." Of course, the status of tap water, which is treated with chlorine or other chemicals, can be easily imagined.

People's Consciousness Changes Water

During the course of sampling and photographing different types of water, it seemed to me that the quality of the water crystals depended on more than just whether it was natural or tap water. I came up with a hypothesis: "Water shows different shapes of ice crystals depending on the information it has received."

I was certain that the difference in ice-crystal formation was not due solely to the presence or absence of chlorine but to the other information affecting it.

To test this, I put water into two glass bottles. On one bottle, I pasted a label typed "Thank you," and on the other, "You fool," in such a way that water would be able to "read" them. The water in both bottles was the same. (See figure 1.4.) I then froze the water in each bottle.

The results were more than supportive of my theory; the water in the bottle with "Thank you" formed beautiful hexagonal crystals, while the one with "You fool" had only fragments of crystals.

If water collects information and its crystals reflect those characteristics, it means that the quality of water changes based on the information it receives. In other words, the information we give to water changes its quality.

I was more motivated than ever to study water, and at the same time, I started to think about how people would be able to become happy with good water.

Water Understands Words
As this experiment convinced me that my theory was correct, we then began to give water various information, freeze it, and photograph the crystals. The results were very interesting.

We consistently found that water responded to positive words by forming beautiful crystals. As if it wanted to express its joyous feeling, the crystals opened up like a flower. In contrast, when water was shown negative words, it did not form crystals.

For example, when we showed water the word "happiness," it formed crystals with well-balanced shapes like beautifully cut diamonds. On the other hand, water exposed to the word "unhappiness" resulted in broken and unbalanced crystals. That water seemed to have tried hard to form crystals, but it exhausted its strength and crashed, happiness slipping away from it.

We continued to show a pair of opposite words to the same water: "well done" versus "no good," "like" versus "dislike," "power" versus "powerless," "angel" versus "devil," and "peace" versus "war." Water formed crystals only when it was shown the positive words.

Interestingly, water responded to foreign words in a similar but not exact manner as it did to Japanese words. Water formed beautiful crystals to all the words expressing gratitude all over the world, such as *thank you* (English), *duoxie* (Chinese), *merci* (French), *danke* (German), *grazie* (Italian), and *kamusamunida* (Korean). (See figure 1.5.)

Water seems to correctly understand the essence of what it was shown—in this case, the feeling of gratitude—and take the information in. Water didn't recognize the word it saw as a simple design; rather, it understood the meaning of it. When water realized that the word carried good information, it formed crystals. Perhaps water is also capable of sensing the heart of the person who wrote the word.

As we were exposing water to lots of words and taking photographs of the resulting crystals, my eyes were glued to one photo, more beautiful than any other water-crystal pictures I had seen. I was fascinated by its beauty.

The crystal was opened up strongly as if a fully blossoming flower. It was as if the water was stretching its hands fully expressing its joy. The words we had shown to the water were "love and gratitude."

Since then, we have talked to water with many kind words, showed it beautiful pictures, and played wonderful healing music, but we have never again been able to take water-crystal pictures as beautiful as the one that resulted from showing water the words "love and gratitude." (See figure 1.6.)

To water, the words "love and gratitude" must be the best information.

We Are Water

In my research, it became clear that water improves or deteriorates reflecting the information it takes in.

This led me to believe that we human beings are also affected by the information we take in, because 70 percent of an adult's body is water.

At human conception, a fertilized egg is 96 percent water. At birth, a baby is 80 percent water. As the child matures, the percentage drops, and it stabilizes at about 70 percent when the individual reaches adulthood. In other words, we live our lives mostly as water. The essence of a human being is water.

We can also say that our lives begin with water and end with water. A fetus developing in a mother's womb echoes our own evolutionary process—from our origins in the sea to the present human form. The amniotic fluid has similar components to sea water. The fetus awaits its time to be born in the mother's sea, breathing through the umbilical cord and placenta.

Water also plays an important role when we die. In Japan we have the custom of giving water to the dying person. Using cotton balls or Shikimi tree leaves, we moisten the dying person's lips. This practice is accompanied by a prayer to bring the dying person's life back. This is the custom based on the understanding that water is the source of our life.

When we photograph water in our research, crystals do not appear immediately after it is frozen. In the microscope, we can observe the process of crystal formation. Crystals grow little by little and complete their formation in one to two minutes, not unlike flowers opening up. The total time for a crystal to appear, grow, and disappear is two minutes. To me, this process symbolizes the preciousness of life. A child grows to become an adult. After maturity, he or she eventually dissipates and disappears. Certainly, water is reflecting life itself.

Since the quality of water improves or deteriorates depending on the information given to it, the corollary for humans, who are made up primarily of water, is to take in good information. When we do, our mind and body can become healthier. Conversely, when we take in negative information, we can get sick.

In essence, we are water. By taking in good water, we can expect to maintain our health. However, good, pure water has become a precious commodity. The previous century experienced many wars over fire, namely, oil. Some people predict that this century will have battles over water. During the twentieth century, the age of fire, we kept the fire going to produce large quantities of energy. In 1900, the earth's population was 1.5 billion. By 2000 that number had grown to 6 billion. Naturally, we needed enormous energy to support the lives of this increased population. Thus, we continuously burned coal and oil. Their toxic by-products eventually contaminated the earth's atmosphere, spreading over the Northern Hemisphere. Polluted rainwater fell from the sky and seeped deep into the earth.

Water circulation occurs in thirty- to fifty-year cycles. This means that rainwater which fell thirty to fifty years ago is now used as groundwater for drinking. As the world's industrial output increased tremendously after World War II, air quality began to seriously suffer. Sixty years after the war, we have no choice but to use polluted water for some time.

Good water may soon be scarce in the world, and bitter battles over precious water resources may be inevitable. These battles could possibly ignite a large-scale world war. But how meaningful would it be to obtain good water after fighting over it? Even if the water was somehow unpolluted, it would contain the negative information from the fighting undertaken to obtain it. In our experiments, we found that water could not form crystals after being shown the word "war."

There Is Hope
If the future I am painting here sounds frightening, here is one reason for hope: If the quality of rainwater in Japan is any indication, the environment has an enormous ability to heal itself when we are kind to it and pay attention to issues surrounding pollution.

As far as my studies go, the quality of rainwater has certainly been improved compared to only a few years ago. While the groundwater is deteriorating, the rainwater is improving.

Some years ago, we collected the rainwater in various cities in Japan and took water-crystal pictures. A few years later, we repeated the process and compared the results. The first time, we couldn't take beautiful pictures of the rainwater in any of the cities—Biei in the tranquil rural area of Hokkaido, Sendai, Tokorozawa of Saitama Prefecture, Asakusabashi in Tokyo, Osaka, and Fukuoka. If pressed, I would say that the rainwater from Osaka formed a shape somewhat close to a crystal.

Biei is located in a beautiful rural region, but the quality of the rainwater there wasn't good. This was understandable because even if the landscape is beautiful, the ozone layer of the sky above Hokkaido was disrupted and the region was damaged largely by acid rain.

However, when we took the rainwater samples a few years later, the rainwater of all the cities except Asakusabashi in Tokyo showed crystals. I was especially surprised to see the differences in the pictures of the rainwater from Tokorozawa; previously it showed only a grotesque shape, but the recent one had a very clear hexagonal crystal.

Although the rainwater collected in Tokyo didn't form a complete crystal, it was in the process of forming it. Unfortunately, it looked as if exhaustion kept the water from completing the crystallization process. Nevertheless, it was trying. (See figure 1.7.)

In other words, the quality of the rainwater all over Japan has improved significantly over the past few years. It is no surprise, because people have started to talk about environmental issues and make unprecedented efforts to improve conditions. As a result, the air has improved greatly within only a few years. In the past, the rainwater was contaminated as it fell through the dirty air. Lately, the air has become cleaner; therefore, the rainwater can come down to the ground without being contaminated. It is certainly an encouraging sign to be welcomed.

Because the water cycle takes thirty to fifty years, it will be a while until the current improved rainwater becomes available for us to drink. We must be prepared to see our groundwater deteriorate for several decades before it starts to get better. However, this example gives us reason to seriously tackle environmental problems, for the sake of the earth and our descendants.

Let's remember that the water exposed to "love and gratitude" created beautiful crystals. Water presents us with a wonderful means to live our lives well and to maintain a healthy mind and body. Keeping water crystals at the central axis, we'll continue our journey to understand the true power of water.

Getting to Know Water Will Change Your Mind and Body

Water and Hado

Water is sensitive to a subtle form of energy called *hado*. It is this form of energy that affects the quality of water and the shape in which the water crystals form. In my previous book, *The Hidden Messages in Water*, the word *hado* was translated as "wave fluctuation." In this book, I use *hado* to mean all the subtle energy that exists in the universe.

All existing things have vibrations, or hado. This energy is often positive or negative and is easily transmitted to other existing things. The thought "You fool" carries its own hado, which the water absorbs and displays as deformed crystals when frozen. On the other hand, when the water has been exposed to positive thoughts, beautiful crystals are formed that reflect the positive hado. Hado, as you can see, is integrally woven into the implications of water's response to information.

To further illustrate the concept of hado, let me use the example of a tuning fork. Perhaps when you were in elementary school, you experienced hitting a tuning fork with a rubber hammer and wondered how this worked. Here is a brief review. Say we have three tuning forks. Forks 1 and 2 have a frequency of 440 Hz, and Fork 3 of 442 Hz. In other words, Forks 1 and 2 are designed to vibrate 440 times per second, while Fork 3 vibrates 442 times per second.

If you hit Fork 1 with a rubber hammer, Fork 2, which has the same frequency, will immediately give off a sound, but Fork 3 won't. Fork 2 resonates with the vibration of Fork 1, but Fork 3 does not. (See figure 2.1.)

Also, Forks 1 and 2 have the frequency of 440 Hz, which means that the sound they give off is "la" in C Major, or A above middle C. If you produce the sounds do, re, mi, fa, sol, and ti, Forks 1 and 2 will not resonate; they only vibrate to precisely the sound of "la."

This explanation should give you the idea that hado is energy. When two things have the same frequency, they resonate with each other. It is easy to understand, then, that as humans we can freely produce our own hado, and then other things with similar hado can resonate with us. Conversely, we can also resonate with the hado that comes from other items.

Each item has its intrinsic vibration. The term *items* here means everything from molecules that make up materials to atoms that make up molecules and subatomic particles that make up atoms. In other words, each subatomic particle has an intrinsic vibration.

Our mind and body are affected by this depending on what intrinsic vibration we resonate with. In human relations, we often say that we are or are not on the same wavelength with someone. This is also related to vibration and resonance.

In a workplace, you might come across a situation like this: An employee thinks, "I know my boss is a nice person, but we are not on the same wavelength. I find it difficult to deal with him." By the same token, the boss may be feeling, "He is working hard, but I don't like what he does."

The boss and the employee are clearly on different wavelengths. No matter how hard they force themselves to work together, their efforts may be wasted. However, if they turn their efforts to tuning in to each other's hado—thinking things from the other's perspective—they will be able to understand each other.

A typical example of hado at work in human relations is that of a man and a woman who meet and fall in love. When they meet, their hados coincide and a resonance occurs. As long as their hado is not affected by external factors (such as an affair), their relationship will last long. On the other hand, if the hado of one person is disturbed, their speech, behavior, habits, and so on, which were once acceptable, may suddenly become intolerable to the other person and the relationship may come to an end.

That is why hado at the level of subatomic particles affects us.

Hado Medicine

Some time ago I was introduced to a type of radionics device capable of measuring various vibrations of the body at the cellular level. I developed an affinity for the device* and became able to use it beyond the device's intended design, namely, to measure hado. My experience with the hado device led me to realize

---

*Please note that this hado device was originally developed in the United States, but I don't know if it is still manufactured. In Japan, we have several dozen devices that I have imported still in use. These are operated by people I've personally trained and certified. This is not a generic device that could be used by anyone. Currently I am not recruiting students. Therefore, please understand that we are not accepting inquiries about this device.

water's ability to receive information. It also led the way to my study of hado medicine, an alternative medical practice that researchers started to study after having felt the limitations of conventional Western medicine.

Although having a device was helpful in my study of hado medicine, I came to believe that humans are capable of feeling and sending hado as well as the device can measure it, if not better. For example, healers and counselors who can help their patients are considered to have the ability to send good vibrations to correct their patients' abnormal vibrational patterns.

The fundamental principles of hado medicine are vibration and resonance. When the cellular vibrations in different parts of the body are disturbed due to various reasons, our body can make a wrong turn. When this situation occurs, a new external vibration can be given to the disturbed cell so as to resonate with it; thus, its intrinsic vibration is restored. This is hado medicine in a nutshell. How can the vibration be corrected?

A hado is a wave; it has a wave shape of peaks and valleys. When the shape of a wave opposite to the original one—valleys for peaks, and peaks for valleys—is used, the wave can be straightened. (See figure 2.2.) By overlaying a wave with another wave in this manner, its characteristics can be cancelled.

Let me illustrate with a sound wave, an easy-to-understand example of a kind of hado. A sound wave also has peaks and valleys. When the sound wave of an opposite shape is used, the original sound wave is cancelled, and the sound disappears.

"That can't be true," you might think. But there are scientists doing research in creating a quiet environment who are using this attribute.

On April 10, 1991, the evening newspaper *Yomiuri* had an interesting article with this title: "Using a sound silences a noise; using an opposite wave cancels the noise." It reported the results derived from research putting hado principles into practice. The article states as follows:

Dr. Yoshio Yamasaki, Science and Engineering Laboratory of Waseda University, succeeded in his experiment to create a quiet soundless space in a room filled with music. This is a new silencing method using canceling sound that counteracts noise. It is expected to be useful to apply to karaoke bars and offices. It may be possible to create a quiet space near a telephone in an office.

Be it music or human voice, each has an intrinsic wave. The basic principle of this new silencing method is to examine the wave shape of peaks and valleys of a sound to be silenced and produce a sound that has the opposite wave shape of peaks and valleys.

The experiment was conducted in a room of seven tatami mats (126 square feet). They analyzed the wave shape of music from one speaker and created the opposite wave shape to the original sound through two other speakers to study the silencing effects.

The result was that the sound disappeared completely at the targeted spot. At the site a couple inches away from the targeted spot, the major components of male voices and music sounds, which are lower than several hundred Hertz, were also cut. By increasing the number of silencing speakers, it is expected to be able to expand the soundless area.

These results were presented at the International Symposium on Active Control of Sound and Vibration, which began on April 9, 1991, in Tokyo. Dr. Yamasaki commented, "This is a method to use sounds to silence sounds. When you make a telephone call, it is sufficient to silence only a limited area. I think that this method can be applied to many other situations."

It is my understanding that this method has also been applied to silence the engine noise of automobiles and reduce the noise from trains and factories.

This principle of canceling the characteristic of the original wave by overlaying an opposite wave shape is not limited to sound waves. It is applicable to all hado. Hado medicine utilizes this concept to restore the patient's health by sending the hado that can cancel his/her unfavorable hado. Water is an integral component, as you'll see.

Through my lectures and writing, I am actively promoting the concept of hado. However, as I am currently too busy writing and speaking to conduct hado testing, I have not been personally involved in measuring people's hado using the hado instrument and helping them restore their health. (I now have twenty practitioners, formerly my students, who provide the services throughout Japan.)

To help a person treat himself or herself with hado medicine, we examine the individual's hado using the hado measuring device. After understanding the disturbances to his or her own vibration, we prepare the water on which the information to correct the vibration was transferred through the hado measuring device. The hado water created in this manner penetrates into the molecules, atoms, and subatomic particles that make up the person's body and stops the disturbances of this vibration. By drinking this hado water, the individual could correct the disturbed vibration. I have used the instrument to measure thousands of people's hado.

The Truth in "Worry Is Often the Cause of Illness"

Through my studies, I noticed many common characteristics that diseased people share and discovered the close correlation between people's emotions and affected parts of their body.

In 1995, I conducted hado examinations on one hundred people. I measured their hado regarding the most commonly shared emotions (thirty-eight traits including stress, worry, pressure, irritability, perplexity, and excess fear) and then checked which part of their body resonated the most with each emotion. Table 1, which follows, shows the results.

For example, those who feel stress tend to have problems with their intestines. Worries are often expressed as problems in the cervical nerves, irritabilities in the parasympathetic division of the autonomic nerve system, excess fear in the kidneys, and anxiety in the stomach.

You might want to think about your present emotions and physical conditions. Do they agree with these findings? It's true that "Worry is often the cause

Table 1. Hado relations between emotions and the body parts

	Main organs that resonate with emotions of disease	Hado of disease	Canceling emotions
Stress	Intestines	Indigestion	Relaxation
Worry	Cervical nerves	Stiff shoulders	Easygoingness
Irritability	Parasympathetic nerves	Insomnia	Calmness
Perplexity	Autonomic nerves	Low-back pain	Good grace
Excess fear	Kidneys	Renal diseases	Peace of mind
Anxiety	Stomach	Dyspepsia	Relief
Anger	Liver	Hepatitis	Compassion
Apathy	Spine	Weakened vitality	Passion
Impatience	Pancreas	Diabetes	Tolerance
Loneliness	Brain's hippocampus	Senile dementia	Pleasure
Sadness	Blood	Leukemia	Joy
Grudge	Skin	Skin ulceration	Gratitude

of illness." When your emotional conditions improve, your illness often moves toward recovery.

In the medical field, they often talk about the "placebo effect." To test the efficacy of a new drug, pharmaceutical companies work together with medical doctors to conduct clinical studies. A conventional method is to have two groups of patients. One group of patients is given the new drug. The other group is told that they are taking the new drug, but actually they are given a placebo (a non-drug, often a simple vitamin).

It is understandable that the people in the group given the real drug get better due to its effect, but many people in the placebo group also get better. Of course, the degree of improvement in the placebo group is often less than in the group with the drug. However, modern medical science cannot explain precisely how people get better just by taking capsules of a placebo.

There is no doubt that when we have an attitude of positive thinking, our health often improves.

Try saying an antonym of the unfavorable emotion that you are feeling. If you are feeling "stress," the antonym is "relaxing," and for "irritability," it is "calmness." The most basic solution to correct your hado is to use the opposite word. To take this approach further, write the antonyms on a sheet of paper and show it to water. The information is given to the water; in other words, the hado of the positive trait is transmitted to the water. Then, when you drink it, you are in effect practicing hado medicine.

In preparation for writing this book, I conducted an experiment by typing the words for various emotions and pasting these labels on bottles of water. Then we froze the water and took photographs of the ice crystals. First we showed the words of negative emotions such as "stress" to water, and took pictures. Then we removed the label and replaced it with its antonym. The results are shown in figure 2.3. I felt that it was exactly "Seeing is believing."

Illness Also Has Hado

From my experience, I have come to some conclusions regarding illness and hado.

A human body has many organs, which are made up of cells. Cells are made up of molecules, and molecules are made up of atoms, and atoms are made up of subatomic particles.

These subatomic particles have their intrinsic hado. When their vibrations are normal, there aren't likely to be any problems. However, if something should happen to cause vibrational disturbances at the subatomic level, this will result in an abnormality. As time continues, the number of subatomic particles with abnormal vibrations may increase, and this in turn will result in disturbing the intrinsic vibrations at the atomic level.

If the number of atoms with disturbed intrinsic vibrations increases, it then disturbs their contributing molecules' intrinsic vibrations. One or two years later, the vibrations of cells can start to be affected. At this point, we may experience some symptoms. Our body tells us about abnormality in the forms of pain, tiredness, and slight fever. Many of us may go to see a doctor at this stage.

Essentially, our body has natural self-healing abilities. Let's say you catch a cold and feel out of sorts. You may get well after staying in bed for a day. Perhaps you are more or less optimistic and good at drawing on your natural healing abilities.

Some people say that they get well just by talking to a doctor. The "placebo effect" may be at work in cases where a doctor they trust says, "It's just a cold, so you should rest well. Don't worry; you will feel better soon." By hearing these words, their anxiety and fear are completely gone. The words awaken their innate self-healing power.

There are others who feel they must go to see a doctor when they have a cold. These people do not get well just by resting, because they tend to become anxious and fearful even when they feel slightly ill. In this situation, the illness that is normally cured by self-healing power may not be cured.

What if you do nothing to correct at the disturbance at the cellular level? What will happen in one to two years when the cellular vibrational disturbance negatively affects the intrinsic vibration of organs? Frightening as it may sound, it can manifest as a chronic disease. From the time of disturbance at the subatomic-particle level, five to ten years may have passed. I believe that each disease of an internal organ has a history of development.

When the abnormality of vibration is enormous, it is not easy to correct it. Therefore, being mindful of our own disturbance of vibration in the early stages and before it gets serious makes it easier to prevent disease by taking corrective actions such as changing our moods. As the saying goes, "Worry is often the cause of illness."

When it comes to correcting the vibrational disruption of disease, conventional Western medicine has its place. After many years of experiments, the clinical efficacy and safety of drugs are confirmed and they are approved for use. I have no intention to deny the effectiveness of such drugs. Doctors prescribe the best medications based on their effectiveness in the past. When we trust and take the medications, our health generally improves.

However, from the perspective of hado principles, it is important to correct the disturbance of intrinsic vibration at the *source*, the subatomic-particle level. Water has the suitable shape to carry various kinds of information. It can get into anywhere to deliver the information. Hado water, then, is capable of carrying hado to the inside of minuscule subatomic particles, whereas the drugs used in Western medicine reach only the cellular level that causes the symptoms. This is the limitation of Western medicine.

In some respect, the drugs used in Western medicine may reach beyond the molecular level. These drugs are designed to mitigate patients' symptoms and, in this sense, are very useful. The sense of relief the patient feels upon taking the drugs can stimulate his or her self-healing ability, and as a result, this might contribute to correcting the vibrational disturbance at the subatomic-particle level. However, the drugs themselves do not directly affect subatomic particles.

I wonder how many doctors understand the way drugs work in terms of vibration. Consider, for example, the use of aspirin for headaches. From the viewpoint of vibration, pain has its own shape of wave. To correct it, we need to send a wave that can cancel the pain. Since the compound of some chemicals and herbs has a wave that can cancel the wave of the symptoms, the pain disappears.

Abnormal hado (many peaks and valleys of the wave) when you have an attack of headache can be cancelled by the hado of aspirin. Therefore, the headache goes away. By matching valleys to the peaks and peaks to the valleys, the sum of pluses and minuses becomes zero.

A human body is said to consist of 60 trillion cells. As these cells fulfill their roles harmoniously, we can live our life healthily. Not only these cells but also molecules, atoms, and subatomic particles have their own intrinsic vibration. When all vibrations go well, our body, as their composite, can work as beautifully as a great orchestra. If a disturbance occurs in a vibration, it creates a discord, and we cannot expect to play beautiful music. This is the reason why treatment at the subatomic-particle level is desirable.

Injuries Are Also Functions of Hado

Besides diseases that affect the organs, we also encounter the troubling matter of injuries. While diseases are internal problems, injuries are external. This difference may sound big; however, from the viewpoint of hado, there is no fundamental difference between the two. Both are caused by a deviation from the intrinsic vibration.

What is an injury? As far as hado principles are concerned, it is the disturbance to an individual's intrinsic vibration due to abnormal vibration given by an external force. A rapid change of vibration may occur to skin cells and bone cells due to a collision, for example. These cells cannot bear the burden of the change, and inflammation or breakage may result. The cells that could not withstand the change may die.

I consider heat (temperature) as an indication of vibrational frequency. To the body that maintains constant vibration, the physical impact of collision, falling, and tumbling can be too great. The moment that an abnormal vibration hits the body, a particular spot may receive it as a very hot stimulus.

So, we often feel hot when we get hurt. The reason we feel the impact as heat is because of the disturbance to the vibration. We can live comfortable lives constantly when our bodily environment is maintained steadily at around the vibration and temperature of 36.5 °C (98.6 °F).

Vibration and living are connected in many different ways. A person is pronounced dead when the heart stops beating. In other words, vibration is life itself. That the kanji character for *life* includes the part meaning *beating* is no coincidence.

In the next chapter I will explain the measuring of hado in more detail, and I will also share stories of how correcting vibrational disturbances in health can lead to remarkable recoveries.

CHAPTER THREE

Water Revives Life Force

Collecting the Information of Illness
With a hado measuring device, we can measure the hado of a person who is feeling ill and send the hado to regulate any abnormal vibration. When the person's own vibration is brought back, the individual can restore his or her health. To put this principle into action, I became an operator of this device to check many people's hado information.

One day, an acquaintance of mine visited me. He said, "This is a hair of my friend's daughter. Could you please analyze it?" He handed the hair to me without telling me anything about her health. Perhaps he wanted to test me on this.

While he waited, I examined the hair using the device. One hour later, I reported what I found:

- The resonance value of the whole brain is extremely low.
- Abnormality in resonance value is observed throughout the body.
- Lead toxin, which is considered to be the cause of these conditions, is observed throughout the body.

After listening to what I had to say, he disclosed the information about his friend's daughter. She had been going to the psychiatric department of a university hospital for the past ten years. Repeatedly she was hospitalized and discharged. She went through detailed examination many times, but no cause was identified.

Since the cause was unknown, her health could not be improved. In despair, her father thought he would try alternative medicine for her, and he asked my acquaintance who introduced my hado medicine to him.

Her father was very concerned about his daughter's poor health. Even though he asked the man to take her hair to me, he did not seem to think much of what the device could do for his daughter.

The next day, I received a telephone call from the man, who excitedly told me that the father became speechless upon hearing the report of lead toxin in the brain. He said, "Come to think of it, we still use lead pipes for our water system in our house."

The father, who had been half-skeptic, brought his wife and daughter to my office the following day. He also brought the tap water from his house. The daughter didn't look like someone who had mental problems. She looked very neat and tidy. Normally, she was fine, but from time to time she would have hallucinations.

With the hado measuring device, I examined the daughter and her parents. Similar to the result from her hair measurement, a very strong lead toxicity was detected in her body. The indicator showed 12/21. The hado device gives the readings as a fraction with a denominator of 21. The ratio is expressed as a numerator. Therefore, 12/21 means the ratio is more than one-half. This is quite a high value. Her parents scored 9/21.

The problem was their tap water. My analysis revealed as high as 19/21, an extremely strong lead-toxicity reaction.

Based on these findings, I told this anxious family, "Her suffering does not seem to be caused by mental problems. I suspect it is due to the lead accumulation in the brain." I will never forget the expressions of the family when they heard me. They looked totally relieved.

It was understandable, because they had finally found that her longtime suffering was not derived from psychiatric problems. They now knew the cause.

The parents decided to replace their lead water pipes immediately. They also asked if I could help remove the lead toxin from their brains using the hado device. I replied, "I cannot be involved in medical treatment. However, I can help you to cancel the hado of lead toxicity, which caused the suffering. In terms of molecular structure, it is simple water; however, I can make the water carry the necessary vibration."

The parents and their daughter accepted my explanation, so I made the hado water that could cancel the lead toxicity for them. The daughter earnestly drank the water for two months. As a result, the initial lead-toxicity level of 12/21 dropped to 2/21.

Possibly as a reaction to her rapid decrease of lead toxicity, the daughter could not sleep at all for four or five nights. However, her health was improved, as was confirmed by her doctor at the university hospital.

This episode has a sequel. While I was pleased to be able to help the daughter, this incident made me realize the power and danger of water.

After the consultation between the parents and me, we asked a public organization to analyze in detail the quality of tap water taken from their water system when it still had lead pipes. Ten days later we received the results. To a certain extent I anticipated the results; the report showed a frightening reality. The tap water of this house was marked "passing," even in the category of lead.

Although the lead was not detected at the molecular level, I believe it was there at the subatomic level. I interpreted this case as a limitation of the current water analysis at the public office.

Water might have not absorbed the toxicity of lead directly; however, it must have taken its hado, which is harmful to us. Water took in the information of lead toxin. As the daughter continued to drink the water with this toxic information, her bodily vibration was disturbed. As a result, she had to suffer mental problems of an unknown origin.

As I mentioned earlier, water carries information. The information can be positive or negative. Since we are water, our body surely responds to the information carried by the water we drink. When we get positive information from water, we become healthier. When we get negative information, we get sick.

People's Names and Pictures Carry the Information of Their Illness

Depending on the information of the words we show to water, water may or may not form ice crystals.

I proved this through taking photographs of water crystals. To substantiate my hypothesis that water changes according to the information given to it, I continued to take photographs of water crystals.

Our common sense tells us it is doubtful that water sees the information and changes itself accordingly. On the other hand, since I had been involved in many experiments using the hado device, I often encountered situations that could not have been explained without this hypothesis. Let me give an example.

Soon after I started to help people restore their health with hado medicine, a man visited me. His friend's twenty-two-year-old daughter had been diagnosed with lymphatic tumor. Her father had died of the same disease several years ago. Furthermore, the father's father also died of the same disease. Both of them were medical doctors. The man came to see me because he was eager to help the daughter somehow.

The young woman was a medical student. She underwent a surgery at her university hospital, and she was still in the hospital for chemotherapy. This put me in a difficult spot. I had been using the hado measuring device to collect the information from the people with disturbed vibrations and making hado water to cancel the disturbances and correct their body's vibration. But how would it be possible to get the information from the person in the hospital? I couldn't possibly take the device to the hospital room. It was hard for me to believe that the medical doctors in this state-of-the-art university hospital would recognize the hado alternative medicine as viable. Even if I was able to bring the device to the hospital, I would be kicked out if they found me. I told this man of my dilemma.

He came back to my office with the patient's mother this time. Both of them appealed to me to measure her daughter's hado. I was touched by their perseverance, and I felt that I must measure her hado somehow and make hado water for her. Suddenly, an idea came to me.

"Could you please take a photograph of your daughter and bring it to me?" I asked. As instructed, the mother took her picture and brought it to me. I was able to measure her hado by putting the picture on the hado machine.

Her picture indicated a very strong anxiety. As I mentioned in the previous chapter, anxiety often manifests as stomach problems. The mother commented that her daughter had been having severe nausea lately and was unable to eat. This response encouraged me. I felt confident that I would be able to collect the information about her disease, even if she was not able to come to my office.

Immediately, I prepared the hado water to correct her hado. Her mother continued to bring a new picture each time she came to see me, and I continued to make hado water for her.

In the case of this young lady, there were many disturbances throughout her body due to the side effects of chemotherapy. She drank the hado water that would cancel the unfavorable hado, and her chemotherapy went on smoothly. After several rounds of chemotherapy, she was discharged from the hospital. She went back to her school. I've heard that she is now working as a medical doctor.

Through many experiences similar to this one, I became convinced that water must read the information from pictures and letters and change its quality accordingly.

The wonder of ice-crystal photographs is that they clearly validate my hypothesis. In fact, I also had a hypothesis that names carry information which water can take in. To prove this hypothesis I once conducted an experiment in which various names such as Mother Teresa and Adolph Hitler were written and pasted on bottles of water and then water-crystal pictures were taken. The results were as I expected. The pictures we took reflected the emotions associated with the person of that name. In other words, names also have hado. I even included these pictures in my photographic books in the past. However, lately I have refrained from taking such pictures, because even if another individual happens to have the same name as a criminal, it doesn't mean that this person is also a criminal. So we no longer photograph or publish crystal photographs from people's names.

Hado Consultation for a Girl with Acute Myelocytic Leukemia

On February 24, 1996, I was asked to work with a girl, then fourteen years old, who had been recently attacked by leukemia. It may be a little bit lengthy, but I would like to show you the process of her recovery based on her records. My intention is to present the true power of hado for the reader's deeper understanding.

She was referred by Mr. Noboru Suzuki, a practitioner of alternative medicine, specifically healing with the touch of his hands. Unfortunately, he is deceased now, but he was quite famous in his field. Mr. Suzuki lived in Hokkaido, and we had met several times. We hit it off well, and we often exchanged our information.

Mr. Suzuki contacted me one day and said, "I am currently seeing a girl with leukemia, but she is beyond my scope. Could you please help her?"

I didn't know to what extent I could help her, but I couldn't say no to Mr. Suzuki's request. As she lived in Tokyo, it would be convenient for her to come to my office. So I met her parents, who brought their daughter's picture with them.

According to them, the daughter was not hospitalized yet. Occasionally, she would groan as if she was possessed. They were not sure if it would be good for their daughter to be hospitalized. Her picture was taken at home. Using the picture, I measured her hado.

First, I measured her genetic information. I will come back to this point later with more detail, but there are many cases in which genetic information inherited from ancestors causes abnormality to the individual's own vibration. Therefore, I felt it was necessary to check her genetic information.

This examination revealed a strong fear of cancer. This emotion was negatively affecting the lymphatic glands. I concluded that she needed hado to calm down her fear. Prejudice was another emotion detected in her. This emotion was negatively affecting the spleen. So another hado was needed to cancel the emotion of prejudice. The next emotion to come up was shyness. This had to be removed, as it was negatively affecting her heart. Then sadness followed. In this manner, I examined her genetic information on seventeen items. The results were quite serious.

After finishing the examination on her genetic information, I checked on her current conditions such as lack of appetite, platelet problems, hemoglobin, and spleen. After about three hours of examination, I prepared her hado water and handed it to her parents.

At the same time, I recommended that they take her to a hospital for treatment, as her conditions were quite serious. The next day, her parents took her to a national pediatric hospital for hospitalization. After drinking the hado water, the girl experienced some breathing difficulties. This is one of the common tendencies that people often experience after drinking hado water, but there is no need to worry. I took it as a function of making a turn for the better.

A week later, on March 3, the parents came back to my office with her picture for the second visit. They told me that since her hemoglobin count had dropped, she received a treatment for it at the hospital during the past week. A diuretic drug was also used for her abdominal-fluid accumulation, and the bacteria count was reduced due to antibiotics. She was unable to eat, so she was receiving nutrients through intravenous drip. She was also showing signs of jaundice.

This time, I examined what was the most severe at present, which happened to be strong fear and sadness. I prepared the hado water to cancel these emotions.

I had her take the hado water five times a day. As she was not in the condition that she could drink it from a glass, her parents gave it to her by dropping one to two milliliters of it under her tongue at a time using a syringe. If a person can drink water, I usually ask him or her to dilute the hado water and to drink it five time daily totaling 800 to 1,000 milliliters a day.

When her parents came back for the third visit on March 7, they brought me good news. The new hado water had seemed to work well for her. The examination conducted on the 5th showed that her white blood cell count dropped from as high as 2,300 to 900. Her jaundice had disappeared, and the functions of her lungs and heart had improved.

However, she had fluid accumulation around the heart, and she was also suffering from anemia. So I prepared yet another hado water for her.

After drinking this water, she started to improve more rapidly. The fluid around the heart was reduced, and she no longer needed intravenous drips in her right arm and leg. Up until that time, she had had intravenous drips in three places, but now she needed it only in her left arm.

As we repeated the process of preparing hado water for her to drink and reexamined her new conditions to make new hado water, her white blood cell count improved. She was allowed to go home

Figure 1.1
Photographing a water crystal that appears at about −15°C (5°F) and disappears in twenty to thirty seconds

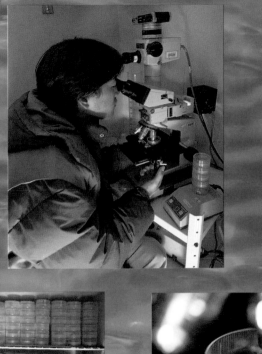

Photographing in a chilled room at −5°C (23°F) requires winter clothes (top). A water sample is dropped onto fifty petri dishes and frozen in a freezer (bottom left). The very edge of the surface of the ice is photographed (bottom right).

Figure 1.2
Tap water

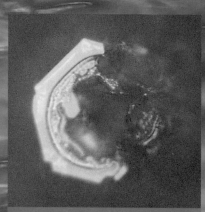

Tap water in Sendai, Miyagi

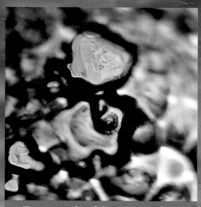

Tap water in Shinagawa, Tokyo

Tap water in Katano, Osaka

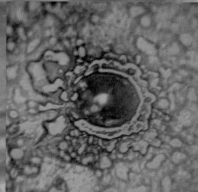

Tap water in Kanazawa, Ishikawa

The results were not favorable except for the water in Katano City. However, some samples looked like they were trying hard to form crystals.

Figure 1.2 (*continued*)

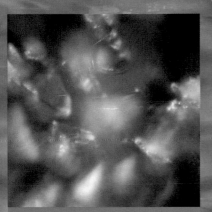

Tap water in Venice

Tap water in London

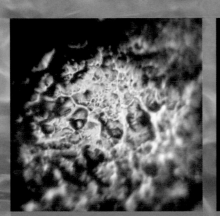

Tap water in Bangkok

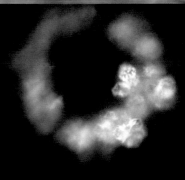

Tap water in Hong Kong

Even in Venice, the water capital, tap water did not form a crystal. The crystal formed from Hong Kong tap water looked blurred. Compared to the tap water in Japan, the water in these two cities looked a little better.

Figure 1.2 (*continued*)

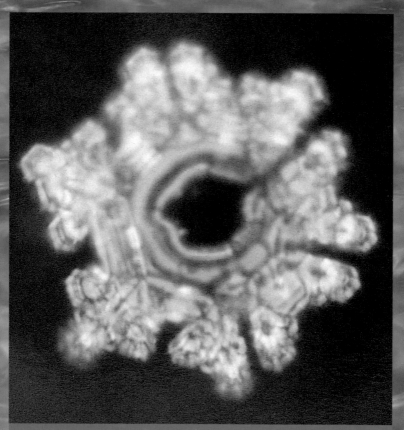

Tap water in Vancouver

Vancouver is located on the West Coast of North America. This city is known for its relatively moderate climate and abundant water sources. Its tap water resulted in a beautiful crystal.

Figure 1.3
Water crystals of some mineral waters sold in the market

Domestic mineral water #1

A brand of domestic mineral water resulted in a very beautiful crystal. It may be the manifestation of its water source's beauty.

Figure 1.3 (*continued*)

Domestic mineral water #2

Another brand of domestic mineral water also formed a fine crystal. This reminded us of the expression "The unity of our body and the land."

Figure 1.3 (*continued*)

A brand of foreign mineral water

This brand, often seen at supermarkets and convenience stores, failed to form a crystal. It made us wonder...

Figure 1.4
Positive language makes a water crystal beautiful

Thank you

We typed Arigato (thank you) using a word processor and pasted it on a bottle of water. An ice crystal of hexagonal shape appeared in the photograph we took.

Figure 1.4 (*continued*)

On a bottle of water, we pasted the Japanese word for "You fool." After leaving it overnight, we then froze the water and phtographed the crystal.

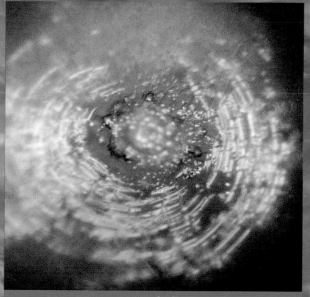

You fool

When we are called something like this, we feel bad. Although we used the same base water as we did for "Thank you," the water with "You fool" resulted in the shape as shown here.

Figure 1.4 (*continued*)

Happiness
We showed the word "happiness" to water. This crystal reminded us of a beautifully cut diamond.

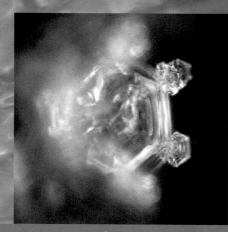

Unhappiness
The water with the word "unhappiness" formed an incomplete crystal. It looked like the water was working hard to make the crystal but failed in exhaustion.

Figure 1.4 (*continued*)

Well done
The water seemed to be pleased when compli-
mented. With its shape stretching freely, the crystal
seemed to communicate its delight.

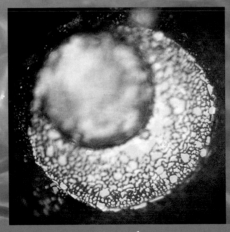

No good
This crystal looked like it had a hole in its heart in
disappointment. Although we tend to use this
expression unconsciously, the crystal reminded us
of its effect.

Figure 1.5
Gratitude has no language barrier

Merci

Kamusamunida
("Thank you" in Korean)

Thank you

The difference in shape of these crystals was perhaps the reflection of the words' origins. The crystal with the Korean letters resulted in a unique shape.

62

Figure 1.6
Let's live our lives with this beauty always in our heart

Love and gratitude

We have taken innumerous water-crystal pictures, but I will never forget how deeply I was touched when I saw this one. Hopefully, we can live life full of love and gratitude.

Figure 1.7
Beautification of rainwater depends on our efforts

1998

Although this town is located in a beautiful area, the rainwater in the past yielded only an ugly shape. Three years later, the rainwater formed a splendid crystal.

Rainwater in Biei, Hokkaido

2001

Figure 1.7 (*continued*)

No other city had such a dramatic change in water crystals as Tokorozawa. It was as if the water listened to the prayer of Tokorozawa residents for improving the environment.

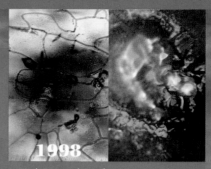

1998

Rainwater in Tokorozawa, Saitama

2001

Figure 1.7 (*continued*)

1998

Rainwater in Taito, Tokyo

Currently, my office is in Taito Ward in Tokyo. It seemed that the rainwater was trying hard to make a crystal. I feel hopeful for the future.

2001

Figure 1.7 (*continued*)

The Waterworks Bureau of Osaka City invested 75 billion yen (US$73 million) in its water-purification project using ozone and activated carbon, which was completed in March 2003. The rainwater may be the reflection of its people's high consciousness.

Rainwater in Osaka, Osaka

Figure 2.1
Tuning forks

When the right tuning fork of 440 Hz is hit with a rubber hammer, the one in the middle with the same frequency resonates, but the one on the left (of 442 Hz) doesn't.

Figure 2.2
Hado and the pattern of its canceling wave

Example of a hado wave pattern

The pattern of the canceling wave for the above

Figure 2.3
The truth in "Worry is often the cause of illness"

Stress
The word "stress" was pasted on a bottle of water. The crystal gave us an impression of being suppressed and shrunk.

Figure 2.3 (*continued*)

Stress ➔ Relax
The label "stress" was removed and replaced by "relax." The crystal seemed unconstrained. As this overlapping crystal indicates, when we are relaxed, people come near us naturally.

Figure 2.3 (*continued*)

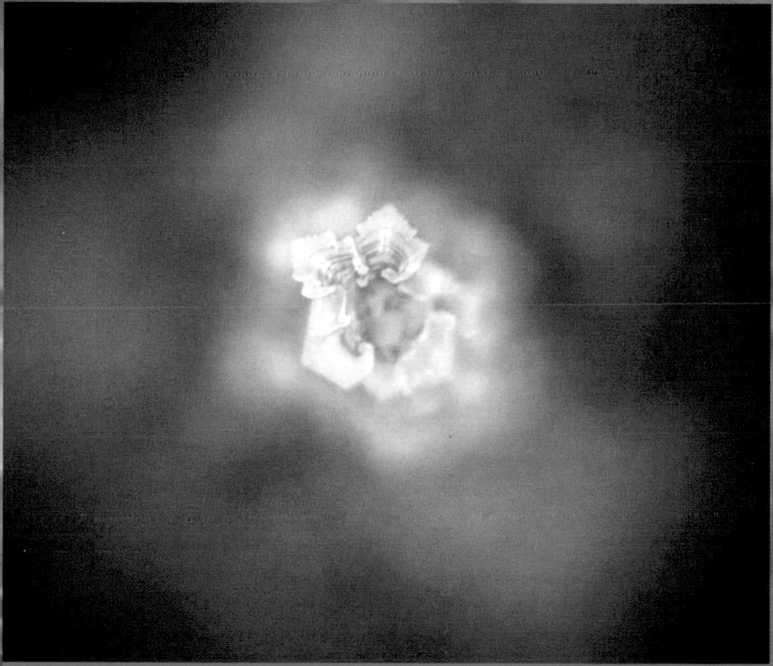

Worrying

The water crystal after being shown "worrying" had a shape similar to the one with "stress." The photograph gives us an impression of withdrawing into its shell.

Figure 2.3 (*continued*)

Worrying ➔ Easygoing
The label "worrying" was replaced by "easygoing." The water crystal was unrestrained and beautiful. This picture tells us the importance of "easygoing," which is *kiraku* in Japanese, meaning literally "enjoying ki" (subtle energy).

Figure 2.3 (*continued*)

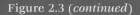

Anxiety

Unexpectedly, this crystal had a good shape. Perhaps the water responded to the original meaning of "anxiety," which is kokoro-kubari in Japanese, meaning "paying attention to." The water understood the kanji letters correctly.

Figure 2.3 (*continued*)

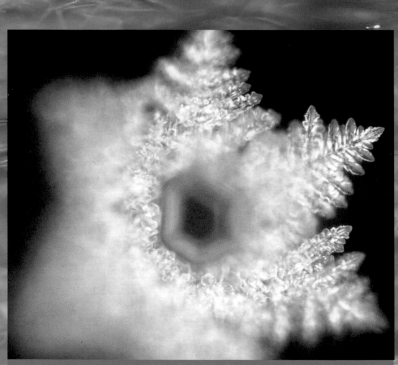

Anxiety ➔ Relief
The label "anxiety" was removed and replaced by "relief." It resulted in a fine-grained crystal. (It looks blurry, because the crystal had a three-dimensional shape. So, focusing on one spot made the rest out of focus.)

Figure 3.1
How did water respond to SARS?

Severe Acute Respiratory Syndrome (Japanese)
We pasted a label written with the Japanese word for "severe acute respiratory syndrome" (SARS) on a bottle of water. The resulting crystals looked shrunk due to terror.

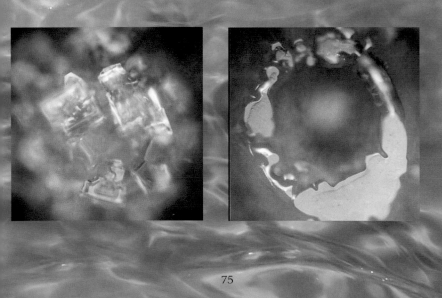

Figure 3.1 (*continued*)

Severe Acute Respiratory Syndrome (Japanese) →
Love and Gratitude (Japanese)
The label "severe acute respiratory syndrome" was removed and
replaced by "love and gratitude." With the energy of "love and gratitude," the water started to shine.

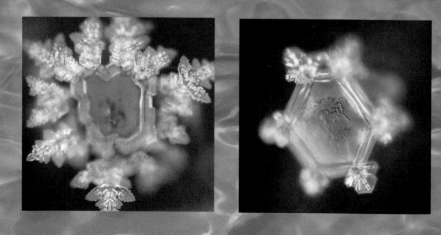

Figure 3.1 (*continued*)

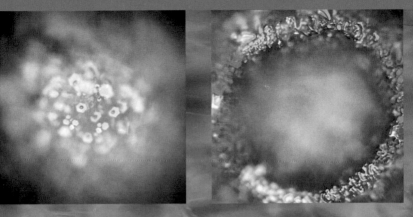

Severe Acute Respiratory Syndrome (English)
We showed the water the spelled-out name for SARS in English. This is
the power of the disease name that terrified the world.

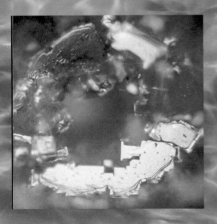

Figure 3.1 (*continued*)

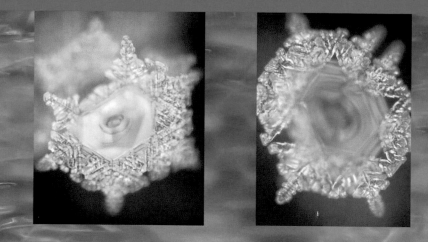

Severe Acute Respiratory Syndrome (English) →
Love and Gratitude (English)
"Love and gratitude" has no language barrier. We showed the water the
words in English; the result was as beautiful as we expected.

Figure 3.2
Cooked rice when spoken to

"You fool" (left)   and "Thank you" (right).

Figure 3.3
People's consciousness changes the dirty water in a dam.

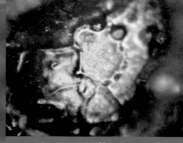

Water at Fujiwara Dam
before the prayer

Water at Fujiwara Dam after the prayer

Before the prayer, the water in the dam was dirty. We sampled the water, whose crystal yielded a shape like a person's face in agony and suffering. We took another photograph of the water after the prayer. The crystal was sparkling with a halo at the center.

Figure 4.1
What happens to water when it is heated in a microwave oven?

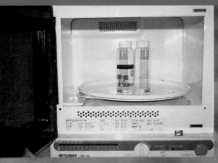

Water heated in a microwave oven
As shown above, we prepared two bottles of distilled water.
One was labeled "love and gratitude," and the other was without a label. We placed them in a microwave oven and heated them for fifteen seconds. Above is the result of the water without a label after being heated.

Figure 4.1 (*continued*)

Water labeled "love and gratitude" heated in
a microwave oven

Just pasting the label "love and gratitude" made a big difference compared to the microwaved water with no label. This
well-balanced crystal gives us a sense of security.

temporarily from April 22 through 29 and again from May 3 through 6. Her parents reported that her facial expression had changed remarkably from a blank look to smiles.

At the same time as she was taking the hado water I prepared, she also received treatments at the hospital. I believe her improvement was derived from both approaches together.

In mid-May, however, she started to experience the side effects of the strong anti-cancer drugs, and she started to lose her hair. It gave quite a shock to this teenage girl. When I examined her conditions the next time, she showed emotions such as loneliness, depression, deep grief, short temper, and severe irritability. Naturally, it takes a long time to counteract this kind of complex emotions. Even if she drank hado water, she wouldn't be returned to health overnight.

Also, there were many disturbances in her body as well. We needed to correct one disturbance at a time, and we continued the process for quite a while. I prepared hado water, and she took it; I made new hado water, and she took it. We repeated this process eleven times.

I will never forget the examination on December 7. It was the day she came to see me in my office for the first time. I had met her only through her pictures; now she was there standing in front of me. It was a very moving meeting.

The previous examination was on September 7, and it had been three months since then. How did her vibration change during this time? I immediately began to use the hado device to collect her information directly. She still had many strong emotions remaining such as fear, panic, fear of losing self-control, suppression, irritability, fear of death, pressure, and stress.

The hado water prepared at that time must have worked really well for her, as her conditions rapidly improved. Surprisingly, she was discharged from the hospital on December 19!

From the beginning of the following year, we examined her once a week. On February 7, she had a menstrual period after having missed it for some time. This bodily change pleased the teenage girl, and she must have felt positive about her illness. In April, she entered high school, and she was able to go to school with her parents' car. Each time we examined her, she showed some disturbance in her vibration, but gradually, it weakened. Finally, we stopped her examination.

This girl is now twenty-four years old. She is working as a designer. Her parents told me recently that she is presently studying how to integrate her techniques as a designer into healing.

Hado Consultation for a Baby with Congenital Heart Disease

Many people have come to see me for consultation. The reason I took on the following case is because the way I met the baby girl was unique, and I conducted the first test for her on July 15, 1994. This baby was referred by her family doctor.

Dr. Y said that he came to visit me because he had read my book and realized the potential of the hado medicine that I had been practicing. On that day, the baby did not come, but the doctor brought her picture, with which I conducted an examination.

The baby's picture was so lovely that she made me smile. I was told that she was at a critical stage because her prognosis was that she might have only a few months to live. In terms of Western medical diagnosis, her condition was not just critical but hopeless.

I felt that the circumstances were bleak, but at the same time my fighting spirit welled up. I told myself that I must protect her life, and I listened to Dr. Y's explanation.

The baby had been diagnosed with a congenital heart disease called infantile heart hypertrophy. As the heart grows abnormally, it occupies more and more space in the chest. Eventually, the disease will kill the infant. In most cases, babies with this disease will not reach their first birthday.

The baby was diagnosed with the disease on May 24. The examination at that time revealed that her heart occupied 68.9 percent of the chest space.

I grew impatient, because I realized that she had only three months before she turned one year old. I was confident about hado medicine, but could I help her in time?

As I mentioned earlier, disease is the result of vibrational disturbance at the subatomic-particle level triggering the disturbance at the atomic level, which in turn causes the disturbance at the molecular level, then the cellular level, and finally at the level of the organs. To correct the vibration with hado water, the process has to be carried out in the reverse order. It takes time. In fact, we have experienced cases where we could not help people because of the time shortage. I had no time to waste. So I started to measure her vibration right away using her picture.

At her genetic level, the hado device detected fear of death, guilt, depression, distrust, and deep grief. I prepared hado water to cancel these emotions.

The second visit was on September 8, two months later. During that time, she had been examined at the hospital, and I was told that her heart was now occupying 54 percent of the chest space. Her second hado examination resulted in similar emotions as before.

Although her heart ratio had dropped to 54 percent, the next examination showed an increase to 59 percent. Her progress was far from desirable, but she was able to celebrate her first birthday on October 15.

Her third hado examination revealed lack of patience, apathy, prejudice, stress, extreme fear, pressure, worry, anxiety, loneliness, distrust, suppression, weariness, panic, procrastination, and self-pity.

The hado water prepared at that time must have worked well for her, because her conditions improved to the point where she was discharged from the hospital. Since then, I examined her once a month and prepared the best hado water each time for her. Her heart's hypertrophic tendency gradually decreased, and the ratio went down to 30 percent.

On April 23, 1996, her twenty-fifth examination, I received the best news possible. She had been examined at the hospital a week earlier, and her heart value was normal. This was the last time I saw this patient. Nevertheless, I promised to do my best should she need my help again.

Dr. Y, her family doctor, became more interested in hado medicine. He even contributed to an article for our journal. In the article, he expressed his determination to respect the merits of both Western medicine and hado medicine and to become the bridge between them.

Conditions That Have Been Thought of as Hereditary

Heredity refers to the information transmitted to an individual from his or her father and mother and also from extended ancestors. The ancestors' information is clearly written in a gene. The ancestors' information has various merits, but unfortunately, it also includes demerits.

In the context of disease, the ancestors' negative emotions are transmitted as negative information that often is manifested physically. This is the reason why I often start with examining the patient's genetic information when I conduct a hado examination.

People often use the term "a family line of cancer." Perhaps such a family had carried the emotions that were likely to cause cancer generation after generation. This is how I understand "heredity."

Except for diseases caused by viruses and electromagnetic waves, the method of hado medicine takes time because we have to correctly understand the patient's genetic information and to cancel its effects one by one. The information of many generations is stored in layers. I believe that there are twelve layers in the human body. We have to go through layer by layer to counteract the information that can trigger a disease.

Many years ago, a couple who attended my seminar told me that their second daughter was suffering from a progressive type of colon cancer. Medical care, including hado medicine, tackled her case wholeheartedly, and the progress of her cancer had been stopped.

Three years later, their first daughter was diagnosed with brain cancer. In a short time period, both of their daughters had been attacked by cancer. The parents were deeply discouraged. The negative emotions of the people around them would not help the patients get well. We decided to constructively examine her hado.

I was worried about how I should tell her parents about the results of the genetic information obtained from the hado measuring device. If I simply said to them, "Negative information was transmitted from a previous life," I might end up confusing them unnecessarily. So I didn't think it was necessary to tell them the detailed information about the examination and its results, and I gave them the minimum amount of information.

Her father, who left my office after having listened to what I said, came back again soon and said, "Well, I am wondering if what you said happens to be the same thing that is written here." He showed me a thick copy taken from an academic journal. It was titled, "The dawn of fulfillment in life: How does the progress of scientific research on reincarnation influence one's view of life?" This article was written by Dr. Fumihiko Iida, assistant professor at Fukushima University, Economics Department.

By just reading the subheadings of the article, I realized that what Dr. Iida was intending to communicate was the same as what I wanted to say.

"That's right. That's right. This is what I meant. Well, Fukushima University is a reputable national university. Time has certainly changed, hasn't it? Now a professor of such a university is boldly presenting this kind of paper in an academic journal!"

I couldn't help but feel astonished to see his paper published fearlessly in Japan, where only Western medicine is regarded highly.

Illnesses React to Negative Emotions

How important it is to live our life positively!

I am quite an optimist. I have been very busy since I started my research. Especially, during the past few years, I have had only five days or less of vacation a year. Suddenly, I find myself having become sixty years old.

In the society where I live, I am old enough to retire from work; however, I have no intention to retire from my active life. Fortunately, I receive many requests for lecturing from numerous countries throughout the world. In spite of frequent traveling around the world to speak, I feel that my physical strength is good enough to beat even a younger person.

The very source of my physical strength is my positive attitude. Conversely, those who think negatively tend to become ill easily. In fact, many of the people who came to see me for hado treatments were those who somehow had lost their balance in a negative direction. The reason was often that negative thoughts resonated with negative factors, such as viruses, and invited them in.

By the end of the 1980s, I had been thinking that the emotion of loneliness was related to the hippocampus of the brain responsible for memories. I was also thinking that aluminum was related to dementia. Through my analysis using the hado measuring device, I was convinced that there were strong correlations between them.

The negative emotion of loneliness affects the hippocampus. Thus, the intrinsic vibration of the hippocampus is disturbed. I found that the frequency of the hippocampus's disturbed vibration resonated with the frequency of aluminum's vibration. I thought that it was because excess aluminum was accumulated at the hippocampus that memories were affected.

Subsequently, the Alzheimer's Association of America and other researchers published papers on the connection between aluminum and Alzheimer's disease.

Also, negative emotions often resonate with viruses. Let's take a cold as an example. At an elementary school, one class is forced to close due to a raging cold. Yet another class at the same school does not have many absent children, and most of them are studying hard. Such a situation often arises.

One of the causes for a cold is a virus. If that is the case, shouldn't the risk of catching the cold be the same throughout the school? Why is it not so? I believe the key to the answer is group consciousness.

Class A has many children who tend to think negatively. Since they heard the news that the cold this year was going to be severe, they think about the cold all the time and wonder how horrible it is going to be if they catch the cold. Influenced by these children, the others also start to think about the cold. On the other hand, Class B happens to have many optimistic children, and nobody thinks about the cold. They are remembering the fun television programs they watched the night before or they are feeling that they can hardly wait for lunchtime to come.

Which class is more likely to have more sick children, Class A or Class B? The answer should be obvious. The kanji character meaning *infection* consists of two characters: *feeling* and *being tainted*.

Negative thoughts resonate with the more negative factors to make the situation worse. This is not limited only to diseases. People often commit suicide after having read some sort of suicidal material. About twenty years ago, a teen idol in Japan committed suicide. Soon after this news was spread, many youngsters followed her lead. And once an incident of a phantom killer occurs, it seems to affect others to do the same.

An ultimate example would be airplane accidents. Why do airplane accidents occur in clusters? It is possible that the anxiety of pilots, mechanics, and passengers merges to form a huge hado and that triggers the next accident?

To live a healthy life, keep your thoughts positive. I am not a medical doctor, but I believe that all doctors should be philosophers as well as healers. The doctor's deep insight and compassion heals patients.

When patients can remove their negative emotions, they will be able to draw upon their own self-healing abilities. In olden times, the doctors were those who were deeply involved in religion, such as priests and shamans. As they did in the past, if doctors can help their patients heal and attain peace of mind, the patients' resonance with diseases would cease.

Why SARS Occurred

A few years ago, a new virus that humans had never encountered before was rampant. It was called SARS (severe acute respiratory syndrome).

Honestly, I felt that this virus had been foreseen. I viewed it as a virus that came into existence because of the weakened state of the earth.

As I mentioned in chapter 1, the world's population was approximately 1.5 billion in 1900. Now it is over 6 billion. The world population in 1 A.D. was believed to be 180 million. This means that the population grew by only 1.3 billion during 1,900 years, while it increased by as much as 4.5 billion during the past one hundred years. Undoubtedly, this is astonishing.

If we view the earth as one living body, we can understand that this gigantic body is suffering from disturbed vibration due to the explosive increase of population. If the earth is compared to a human body, the disturbance to its vibration must have progressed beyond the disturbance at the subatomic particle, atomic, or molecular levels. Perhaps it has already reached to the cellular level, or even the vibration of organs may have been affected.

Therefore, we must realize that the earth's immunity and self-healing power has been reduced tremendously. When the lowered immunity is coupled with negative emotions of social anxiety, it is easy to resonate with a virus that has the same frequency.

In 2003, while people in Canada were being infected with SARS and loss of life, I visited the country, including Toronto, the most severely affected city. While I was there, an idea came to me.

I contacted my office in Tokyo and instructed them to take new water-crystal photographs. I was wondering what would happen if we showed the words "severe acute respiratory syndrome" both in Japanese and English to a bottle of distilled water.

Normally, distilled water would form crystals. In fact, before we showed the words to the water, it formed crystals. What happened to the water after having shown it these words?

As expected, after water was exposed to these words in both Japanese and English, it formed only eerie shapes, far from beautiful crystals. The name of the disease contained negative information strong enough to prevent the distilled water from making crystals.

After we finished this experiment, we decided to conduct yet another experiment. We gave a new piece of information to the same water that had changed its quality after having been exposed to the name of the disease. This time the information was positive in nature.

We removed the paper "severe acute respiratory syndrome" from the bottle and replaced it with the label "love and gratitude." We did this in both Japanese and English.

As a result, the water formed crystals again. Both water samples given the information in Japanese and in English produced beautiful crystals. (See figure 3.1.)

Perhaps there are people who find it hard to believe the results we present here and who may say, "It must be a simple coincidence" or "You must be lying." However, it is an undeniable fact. The water changed dramatically according to the information exposed to it.

Giving Attention Is a Way of Giving Energy

Because the following case was introduced in my book *The Hidden Messages in Water* (Beyond Words Publishing, 2004), some readers may remember it. Here I quote from this book:

> A family that subscribed to our magazine conducted an interesting experiment. They put rice in two glass jars, and every day for a month said "Thank you" to one jar and "You fool" to the other, and then they tracked how the rice changed over the period. Even the

children, when they got home from school, would speak these words to the jars of rice.

After a month, the rice that was told "Thank you" started to ferment, with a mellow smell like that of malt, while the rice that was exposed to "You fool" rotted and turned black. [See figure 3.2.]

I wrote about this experiment in the book [*Messages from Water*, Vol.1] that I published, and as a result hundreds of families throughout Japan conducted this same experiment for themselves. Everyone reported the same results. One family tried a variation of the experiment: like the others, they said, "Thank you" to the first bottle of rice and "You fool" to the second bottle, and then they prepared a third bottle of rice that they simply ignored.

What do you think happened? The rice that was ignored actually rotted before the rice that was exposed to "You fool." When others tried this same experiment, the results were again the same. It seems that being ridiculed is actually not as damaging as being ignored.

The result of this experiment has a significant meaning. The hardest thing for life is to be ignored and given no attention. To give your attention to something is a way of giving energy. Someone who grows plants told me that if you talk to the plants while watering them, they will grow faster and produce more beautiful flowers. By receiving attention, life can get the energy to move in a better direction.

The same is true with human society. Due to a sluggish economy, restructuring has become a popular practice among many Japanese corporations. The companies mercilessly push employees deemed unnecessary away from the main activities of their business. Still other more heartless companies put them in a restructuring room, and they are not given real jobs. From their perspective, being severely scolded by their boss would be easier to take.

There is no harder situation than being put in a position where you have no work to do and no one talking to you. When they are no longer able to bear such a circumstance, they voluntarily leave the company. The worst-case scenario is that they are driven to commit suicide.

Let's think about the reverse. If we want our employees to do their jobs well, let's talk to them on an ongoing basis to encourage them. If we want to discipline our children, let's say something to them that is positive and inspirational.

If we get sick or injured, let's treat the affected cells kindly. Paying full attention to the affected part will quicken its recovery. We should remember that we have been able to live our life in health because of that part of our body, and we should feel grateful for it.

If people are sick around us, let's say something to them. Realizing that they are making our life richer by their contribution, let's encourage them whole-heartedly with positive words. By doing so, we can expect their quick recovery.

The Power in Our Words

Water is sensitive, and it responds to what we say. When we send good hado to water by saying positive words to it, it will show us beautiful crystals. Also, our prayers send out energy and change the quality of the water. By offering prayers to water, we send hado to the water, and such water gains the power to potentially answer our prayers.

There is a knack to doing this. We can send stronger hado by offering our prayers in the past tense than in the future tense.

For example, let's assume that a child whose mother got cancer says his prayers to water for her recovery: "I hope my mother's cancer will be cured." I am not saying that such a prayer is bad. Definitely, the hado of this prayer affects water. To pray the same thing but using different words can be a more effective way to change water: "My mother's cancer was cured."

Strictly speaking from the grammatical viewpoint, the past tense does not make sense, as the event is yet to happen. However, we can make our thought and intention stronger by saying it in the past tense. Rather than saying it in the future tense, "will be cured," the past tense, "was cured," can communicate our strong will more assertively. When we offer our prayers, it is important to have a strong image of a cure as soon as we state it.

Imaging something means that we are praying for the final result. Let's suppose that we want to become the secretary-general of the United Nations when we grow up. Compared to making this statement in the future tense, by asserting "I became the secretary-general" while we are imagining ourselves thirty or fifty years later chairing a meeting of the United Nations, we can expect to live our life more smoothly. This can be materialized only after an image is formed.

The image I am discussing here is our hope. It is a form of positive information. As we repeat the information with strong words, water will naturally help us. It appears from my experience that loudly vocalizing the words gives off a stronger hado than writing them on paper.

I am not a man of religion, nor do I want to praise religions unnecessarily. However, the prayers used for a long time by a religion have a strong hado energy. I feel that if we believe in our religion faithfully and recite the prayers undoubtedly, we will be blessed with a strong power.

Once I witnessed a man of religion whose prayers caused an enormous amount of water to change. I visited with Chief Priest Houki Kato of a Japanese Esoteric Buddhist temple, as I had heard that he performed incantations and prayers at Fujiwara Dam in Gunma Prefecture. He had been conducting such incantations and prayers a number of times. I have seen the photographs of the dam reservoir at Fujiwara Dam taken before and after his prayers. In comparison, the colors of the two "before" and "after" pictures certainly looked different. As I was greatly interested, I asked Priest Kato if he would let me go with him when he performed his prayers the next time.

Before his prayers started, we collected a sample of water from the reservoir. Priest Kato began his incantations and prayers. He continued to pray for one hour while creating a highly solemn atmosphere around him.

After he finished his prayers, I was listening to his talk. Perhaps it was about fifteen minutes after the prayers ended. The staff who accompanied me exclaimed, "Wow! Look, the color of the reservoir is changing rapidly!"

Indeed, the water of the huge reservoir was getting clearer. Before the prayer, there was no reflection on the surface, as the water was muddy. Now the trees around were reflected on the surface, forming sharp images. We have the word *kotodama* (spirit of words) in Japanese. Most definitely, Priest Kato's words must have had that spirit. I was witnessing the power of spirit in action.

We also collected a sample of water after the prayer to take back to Tokyo, where we were going to take water-crystal pictures.

No matter how often we tried, no crystal was formed from the sample of water before the prayers. On the other hand, the water after the prayers formed a crystal of heavenly beauty. It had a double structure of a small hexagon inside a beautiful outer hexagon. (See figure 3.3.) This crystal is also on the cover of my book *The Hidden Messages in Water*.

"Love and Gratitude" Enhances Immunity

To make "good water," get some distilled water, if possible, to start. We can take beautiful ice-crystal pictures from distilled water without doing anything special to it. This means that the water is good and pure. However, it may not be that easy to get distilled water. In that case, ordinary tap water is acceptable.

Please offer a prayer to the water in the bottle. If we could perform incantations and prayers like Priest

Kato, who changed the reservoir water at Fujiwara Dam, it would be the best. However, it would be difficult for us ordinary people to recite the prayers with "spirit of words" just like he did. Since we haven't received special training, we would be distracted by all of our other thoughts.

So, simply talk to the water. If you have a wish, you might want to say it as an emphatic statement in the past tense, as I explained earlier, while imaging your success.

Ideally, you want to recite your prayers aloud continuously. However, it may not be very practical for today's busy people to recite their prayers to water for a few hours every day. I recommend that you write words on paper and paste it to the container with the words facing in so that the water inside can read them. Additionally, talk to the water from time to time and occasionally shake the bottle, which helps to activate the water and contributes to the vibrations.

By just doing these things, you can make your own personalized hado water. I suggest you drink five glasses of this water every day.

What should you do if you don't have specific wishes? The best thing is to show the words "love and gratitude" to water and talk to it. For a long time, I have been giving water many pieces of information and taking ice-crystal photographs. We have given water as many pieces of positive information as we could think of—beautiful words, beautiful scenery photographs, and beautiful music—in order to take crystal pictures. They were all beautiful, but the most beautiful one to me was the crystal that formed after the water was exposed to the words "love and gratitude."

"Love" is absolute, and "gratitude" is relative. Absoluteness is an active energy, and relativeness is a passive energy.

Only when we have a receiver can we be involved in the act of giving. No matter how hard you try to give your love, without a receiver, you won't be able to do so. It is Nature's providence. The sun is on the side of giving, and the moon is receiving. This is true with male-female love and with the act of giving relating to the birth of life. These acts are also possible when there are receivers.

Splendidly, the water crystals present us Nature's providence and the concept of life's phenomena.

Not just love. Not just gratitude. Only when the two are together can they manifest the workings of Nature.

I came to realize that perhaps there is no better information than these two words carry. The ratio of water is one to two, oxygen to hydrogen. Learning from this structure, I even venture to believe that good water means one portion of love and two portions of gratitude.

CHAPTER FOUR

Using the True Power of Water in Your Life

Eat Foods with Good Hado

We cannot live without water. Water carries vibration, the source of energy.

Some may say, "What about food? We cannot live without food, either." That's right. Indeed, we cannot live without food. Food is important for us, of course, but its vibration is what is essential for living a vital life.

All that lives must continue to vibrate. In other words, each cell must also continue to vibrate.

Vibration cannot continue forever without something causing it. This is the same with everything in life. For example, a top cannot spin indefinitely; it eventually stops if we don't keep it going. To avoid the stoppage, we give the top a sort of shock by turning it with a string. For the vibration of living creatures, food plays this role.

Each food has a certain vibration. Strawberries have their own vibrations, and apples have theirs. Of course, each organ or cell of our body has its own vibration. The vibrations of foods resonate with the vibrations of our organs and cells. Through this resonance of the body's organs and cells, life keeps going. To influence the body's many organs with good vibrations, it is important to eat a variety of foods. From the nutritional viewpoint, we are told to eat various foods to avoid an unbalanced diet. This is because we need to make our organs and cells resonate as much as possible with the vibrations derived from food.

Some time ago, a dietician named Dr. Akiko Sugahara and I conducted research into the hado of food. Dr. Sugahara received her doctorate degree from the University of Tokyo, the Graduate School of Medicine. After having worked at a famous research institute, she established Sugahara Institute. She is regarded as an authority in her field. She became interested in hado because she happened to read one of my books.

Using an instrument to measure hado, we measured the hado of many foods. For partial results from the study, see table 2, which follows.

Table 2. Hado values of food
Hado values of vegetables

	Hado for immunity	Hado for anti-stress	Hado for anti-depression
Spinach	+18	+18	+9
Boiled spinach	+7	+7	+21
Raw molokheiya	+21	+20	+21
Grain molokheiya	+21	+21	+12
Flat yam	+8	+7	+3
Taro	+4	+2	+3
Chinese yam	+19	+10	+8
Garlic	+21	+17	+5
Cabbage	+4	+5	+7
Lettuce	+7	+8	+7
Chinese cabbage	+8	+8	+12
Japanese parsley	+8	+9	+9
Green onion	+10	+10	+12
Mitsuba parsley	+12	+11	+15
Japanese radish root	+15	+14	+12
Japanese radish leaf	+9	+7	+16
Carrot	+14	+14	+15
Burdock root	+13	+12	+20
Lotus root	+18	+18	+11
Shiitake mushroom	+10	+12	+16
Mushroom	+21	+15	+16
Maitake mushroom	+21	+21	+16

As mentioned earlier, the highest measurement we get from this instrument is 21/21. When we measure hado, it is expressed as a fraction with a denominator of 21; however, for the sake of simplicity, I will use only the numerators here.

Table 2 (*continued*)
Hado values of fish and shellfish

	Hado for immunity	Hado for anti-stress	Hado for anti-depression
Abalone	+7	+9	+9
Clam	+16	+12	+15
Turban shell	+20	+20	+20
Shijimi clam	+15	+14	+9
Sea urchin	+16	+16	+16
Octopus	+16	+16	+14
Sea cucumber	+19	+16	+18
Tuna	+12	+5	+12
Wakame root	+19	+19	+20
Dry wakame seaweed	+20	+20	+20
Raw wakame seaweed	+20	+21	+21
Ise hijiki seaweed	+21	+21	+21
Chiba hijiki seaweed	+17	+20	+17

Hado values of meats and egg

		Hado for immunity	Hado for anti-stress	Hado for anti-depression
Beef		+17	+5	−12
Pork		+9	−7	+7
Mutton		+10	+10	+6
Broiler	Meat	+8	−14	+6
	Liver	+10	+0	+13
Local Chicken		+18	+16	+9
Duck		+18	+15	+12
Egg (unfertilized)		+9	−13	+3

We studied hado regarding immunity, anti-stress, and anti-depression. In general, vegetables scored high. In

Table 2 (*continued*)
Hado values of fruits

	Hado for immunity	Hado for anti-stress	Hado for anti-depression
Apple	+14	+14	+14
Fig	+19	+20	+20
Kiwifruit	+18	+19	+18
Yuzu citron	+14	+14	+14
Kumquat	+19	+19	+18
Kyoho grape	+18	+19	+19
Tangerine	+11	+14	+12
Prune	+20	+18	+21

Hado values of nuts and seeds

	Hado for immunity	Hado for anti-stress	Hado for anti-depression
Pine nut	+21	+21	+21
Walnut	+20	+21	+21
Lycium fruit	+20	+20	+20
Ginkgo nut	+19	+20	+19
Pumpkin seed	+18	+18	+18
Cashew nut	+16	+16	+17
Sunflower seed	+21	+21	+21
Sesame seed	+20	+20	+21

other words, they were effective at counteracting disease, stress, and depression. Nevertheless, each vegetable was slightly different. Our results regarding vegetables reinforce the importance of eating a variety of foods.

One noteworthy test was spinach; when it was raw, it had good hado. However, when it was boiled, it lost some of its good qualities. I didn't expect the difference to be so significant. These results also surprised Dr. Sugahara.

Next, we measured the hado of fish and seafood. Overall, they showed good hado. Dr. Sugahara analyzed the results and said that since the sea is the rich repository of minerals, these foods tended to score higher than foods from the land.

Studying meats yielded interesting results. Chicken and duck scored high overall in the categories of immunity, anti-stress, and anti-depression. On the other hand, beef, pork, and mutton were not so good. Especially in the category of anti-stress, there were obvious differences between meats and poultry.

Then we went on to study fruits and nuts. Dr. Sugahara was impressed by the results and commented that nuts, which are often referred to as saints' food, are the best. She had been saying that nuts give us the best nutrients, and her point was verified by our study. (As a side note, although it is not my intention to connect religions with hado, I have noticed that as people go through religious training, they often can sense what would have good hado.)

From the nutritional viewpoint, nuts are believed to have a diuretic effect and to keep blood vessels supple, so they are good for preventing cerebral thrombosis and cerebral hemorrhage.

We then moved on to find out if there would be any changes in hado depending on the methods of cooking. For this study, we picked hamburger. We compared a boil-in-bag hamburger mass-produced in a factory with one homemade. This idea came from Dr. Sugahara; she said, "There may be a difference in hado between a boil-in-bag hamburger and one made at home. The hado of the person who makes it may be a factor. This could lead us to understand the theme, What does the taste of home cooking mean? When we put our whole heart into cooking, I think it can improve hado."

To prove her hypothesis, we conducted the test. We compared four different hamburgers: boil-in-bag, homemade, homemade with loving words spoken to it, and homemade with angry words spoken to it. (See table 3.)

Table 3. Hado values of hamburger preparation methods

	Hado for immunity
Boil-in-bag hamburger	−4
Homemade hamburger	+10
Hamburger with loving words	+16
Hamburger with angry words	−6

The loving words we used were "looks delicious," "smells good," and "can't wait to eat with everyone else." The angry words were "frustrated," "tired," and "why do I have to make such a troublesome dish when I don't have time?"

As anticipated, the results showed differences between a boil-in-bag hamburger and a homemade one. It defied our imagination to learn how much influence the words had on the food. From my past experiments, I was fully aware that water was affected by the information given to it. However, I didn't expect that food would show such a big difference depending on the words spoken to it.

A dish may be made at home, but there is a difference when one makes it with love and when one showers words of abuse on it. As a matter of fact, a boil-in-bag hamburger resulted in better hado scores than hamburger homemade with angry words.

Therefore, I ask people to send love and gratitude when they make meals for their families; I ask family members who taste these dishes to be loving and grateful.

The Rapid Heating of a Microwave Oven Disturbs Hado

We took distilled water that would normally form beautiful crystals and heated it in a microwave oven for fifteen seconds. We could take only grotesque photographs of this water, far from crystals. (See figure 4.1.)

The electromagnetic waves of a microwave oven are quite strong. By exposing water to the waves for just fifteen seconds, the good hado of the distilled water was destroyed completely.

For some time I had been thinking that the rapid change of water temperature would deteriorate the quality of water. My reason for thinking this goes back to the time we were struggling to take our first water-crystal photographs. We used pure, clean water, froze it, and then took pictures. Our trouble was to discover the best length of time for freezing the water. Eventually, we were more likely to find water crystals when we took about three hours to slowly freeze the water. The process to arrive at this finding wasn't easy.

While thinking that shorter freezing time would ensure fewer changes in the quality of water, we tried high-speed freezing by using a state-of-the-art freezer as well as by using liquid nitrogen. However, we found no water crystals after such processes. In order to maintain the water's beautiful qualities, it was necessary to take more time to freeze it. To me this meant that when water is forced to change its temperature rapidly, its quality deteriorates.

A microwave oven is capable of instantly increasing the temperature of an item. After this unnatural process, how did the hado change? In our experiment, we used the same homemade hamburgers and compared three different cooking methods: in a frying pan, in a microwave oven for a normal amount of time (two minutes), and in a microwave oven for an excessive amount of time (three minutes).

The results were not surprising to us. The hado of the hamburger grilled in a frying pan was +10, while the one cooked for a normal amount of time in a microwave oven was +6, and the one cooked for an excessive amount of time in a microwave oven was as low as –2. (See table 4.)

Table 4. Hado values of hamburger cooking methods

	Hado for immunity
Pan grilling, normal	+10
Microwave cooking, normal	+6
Microwave cooking, excess	–2

According to Dr. Sugahara, the difference between the normal and excessive amounts of time in the microwave cooking was only one to three minutes. This amount of time is within the range in which people often make mistakes while cooking. Yet such mistakes could result in crucial differences in terms of hado. This experiment taught me a lesson in how difficult it is to work with electromagnetic waves.

Improve the Hado of Cellular Phones, Televisions, and Personal Computers

I mentioned earlier that the hado of the earth, a living entity, has been disturbed by the rapid population growth. One factor for the planet's disturbed hado must have resulted from the fact that this increased population is using many devices with electromagnetic waves. The devices that produce electromagnetic waves not only affect the hado of the earth negatively but also affect you, the user of the devices, in disturbing your hado and potentially harming your health significantly.

Previously I explained our experiment in which distilled water heated for only fifteen seconds in a microwave oven formed no crystals, although the water would have formed crystals had it not been heated. Hopefully, this has shown you how significant the effects of electromagnetic waves can be. I also have other examples from experiments on cellular phones, television sets, and personal computers.

The first case was with a cellular phone. We put distilled water into a bottle and tied a cellular phone to it with a string. Then we rang the cellular phone and kept the line on in silence for a minute and repeated the process ten times. The next experiment involved a television set. We left a bottle of distilled water next to a television set that was kept on for four hours. Similarly, we put a bottle of distilled water next to a personal computer for four hours.

The results showed horrible effects on the water crystals. Just as with a microwave oven, water exposed to a cellular phone, a television set, and a personal computer did not yield water crystals. The only patterns that appeared were ugly circular shapes. I understood clearly how negatively electromagnetic waves affected the quality of water.

We spend our lives near devices that generate electromagnetic waves, and our bodies' hado is certainly disturbed by them. For instance, when we are exposed to electromagnetic waves for a long time, especially when we do not feel well and our immune system is compromised, a disease process may be triggered.

Then, what should we do? The ideal would be to live our lives without using these devices. At the beginning of the twentieth century, before the explosion of population, the earth was beautiful. There was no massive production and consumption of energy or electromagnetic waves. Should we go back to a lifestyle without microwave ovens, cellular phones, television sets, or personal computers?

No, this isn't realistic. Of course, if you could retreat deep into the mountains and live on air, you could perhaps escape electromagnetic waves.

However, not everyone could afford to quit his or her job and move to the country. What about me? I too use e-mail more and more in business correspondence.

In this day and age, it is difficult to live without using devices that generate electromagnetic waves. Having realized that, what we need to do is to find a way to use these devices wisely. By the way, I have found a wonder drug. Let me share it with you.

The answer was really simple. In chapter 3, I wrote about the water that deteriorated in quality after it was exposed to the words "severe acute respiratory syndrome." The distilled water that would normally form crystals could not do so after we placed a label with "SARS" written on it. However, it revived and formed crystals after the label was replaced by one on which "love and gratitude" was written.

The same was true with the water that was disturbed by electromagnetic waves and that could not form crystals. In addition to the regular samples of distilled water, we prepared bottles of distilled water labeled "love and gratitude" and exposed them to the electromagnetic waves of a microwave oven, a cellular phone, a television set, and a personal computer. In the same conditions as the regular samples, the set of samples with "love and gratitude" were also showered with strong electromagnetic waves.

The water labeled "love and gratitude" showed hardly any negative effects of the waves. Unlike the water in the regular bottles, all of the sampled water labeled "love and gratitude" formed beautiful crystals. (See figure 4.2.)

Stickers or pictures of water crystals shown "love and gratitude" work just as well as the words themselves for protecting water from the bad effects of electromagnetic waves.

Our body is made up of water. We now know how to make water resistant to the effects of electromagnetic waves. This means that we also know how to protect ourselves from these waves.

In order to protect ourselves from the electromagnetic waves generated by the devices we use, we could say "love and gratitude" whenever we use them! This would be a sure method. However, this method is as unrealistic as saying, "Don't use any of these devices." How would it be possible to talk on a cellular phone while reciting "love and gratitude"?

It would be meaningless, if we don't come up with a more realistic method. While I was worrying about it, an interesting idea for an experiment flashed into my mind.

Previous to our experiments with electromagnetic waves, I had seen a documentary program on NHK (Japan's sole public broadcaster) and was deeply moved by the program. The television pictures were beautiful and had some "healing" effects. I remembered this program and thought that if I showed this program to water, it would form crystals while maintaining its quality in spite of its exposure to the electromagnetic waves' bad influence. It would be as resistant to the electromagnetic waves as it was with the words "love and gratitude."

When this idea hit me, I couldn't stand still. As the saying goes, good deeds should be done quickly. I immediately got a videotape of the program and played it on a television set.

The result was as I expected. The water placed near a television set would be negatively affected by the strong electromagnetic waves under normal circumstances, but with this particular program it produced clear crystals. (See figure 4.3.)

The lesson is that positive information can prevail over electromagnetic waves.

If our food is to be cooked in a microwave oven, let's send our "love and gratitude" to the food and to the person who prepares it.

When we use a cellular phone, let us limit our conversations to cheerful topics. If we use the cellular phone for business conversations, let's use it for topics such as closing a deal. To report a failure, it would be better to use a regular phone. If a couple is to converse intimately on a cellular phone, they can perhaps avoid the effect of electromagnetic waves. If the conversation is filled with love, even speaking on a cellular phone for a long time would be all right. However, let's be sure never to talk about separation on a cellular phone. Such a talk would be better done face-to-face.

As for television, let's watch the programs or videos that are healing in nature. While we are watching news on television, we might hear reports of ghastly murders or tragic accidents. In such circumstances, it would be best to change the channel or turn it off.

It is also advisable to avoid programs and movies that include constant violence. In playing video games, it is better to avoid software that promotes fighting. The number of terrible murders by minors has been increasing; I believe they have strayed into the virtual world and have been negatively affected by electromagnetic waves. In this connection, I might add that the result was not good when we showed a pornographic video to water.

When we use a personal computer, we should be mindful. If we are using it for business, let us enjoy our work with enthusiasm and a positive attitude. Our positive attitude will prevail over electromagnetic waves. On the other hand, if we are to grouch by saying "Why do I have to do this?" in our job, the strong electromagnetic waves from the personal computer could disturb our hado.

Good Music Reaches Our Cells

Improving the quality of your water is something you can do yourself. Since we are water, we must avoid disturbing our hado with the water we drink.

Fortunately, as discussed earlier, it has been proven clearly that it is good to give water information of healing and to have positive thoughts for it. Please remember that even water placed near devices that generate strong electromagnetic waves could make crystals when given such information.

What kind of information has a healing effect? I have been talking about the importance of language such as "love and gratitude." However, information is not limited only to words. Other kinds of information also have healing properties for improving water. Being sensitive, water responds to beautiful pictures and music.

As a matter of fact, when we started to take water-crystal photographs, first we conducted an experiment to give water the information of music before we tried one with words. A young researcher who had been fascinated with taking water-crystal photographs said one day, "Let's have water listen to music.

I think there will be interesting water crystals." The idea struck me right away. After all, I am very fond of music. One time, I even seriously thought about becoming a vocalist. So we decided to play pieces of my favorite classical music one after another. (See figure 4.4.)

After trials and errors, we arrived at the following method to play music to water:

1. Place a bottle of water between two speakers and play a piece of music at the normal volume.
2. After the music is finished, tap the bottom of the bottle well to give it some vibration.
3. Leave the bottle there overnight, and then tap it again before putting it into a freezer.

We played music under the same conditions as we would enjoy it. The results defied our expectations. The water showed a reaction similar to the healing effects that we would feel from music. Especially, water made very complex and intricate crystals after it was exposed to the music of a full orchestra.

Perhaps the harmony created by different instruments produces good hado. Our body is made up of as many as sixty trillion cells. Our body is the harmony played by these cells. The harmony of the music played by an orchestra can reach each and every cell of our body and thus contribute to our health.

Besides classical music, we also played so-called healing music to water, and beautiful crystals resulted; on the other hand, when the water listened to heavy-metal music, no crystals were formed. (See figure 4.5.)

I believe that music truly has healing effects. We feel we are healed when we listen to music, perhaps because the water in our body is healed by listening to the music. Good music reaches every one of our sixty trillion cells.

Our success in taking photographs after playing music to water led us to do the subsequent experiments such as showing beautiful pictures to water and having water read the information in words.

For this book, I have selected some pictures taken from our experiments that show which kinds of music seem to have good effects on our body. All of these pieces are popular ones; you might want to listen to them in the morning or during your relaxation time in the evening. (See figure 4.6.)

Lately, I have been thinking more about the relationship between music and our body. In the medical field, there are more and more physicians who incorporate "music therapy" into their practice. They say that having the patient listen to music accelerates the recovery process. I am a great supporter of this therapy. We are water. If the music makes water happy, it must positively affect our cells, which are made up of water.

Furthermore, I am interested in examining each person's hado and creating the sounds that closely match it.

In the past, I measured and examined individuals' hado and created water that contained information to correct their disturbed hado. Each person has his/her intrinsic hado; therefore, the information that water should carry differs for every person. As the water was individualized after having found the most suitable hado for the person, it was very effective. I believe we could do the same with sounds.

Dr. Naoki Shibuya, who established Shibuya Brain Surgery Clinic in Shizuoka City, is known for his practice using "sound-energy therapy." Dr. Shibuya earned a doctorate degree through his research in brain tumors and chemotherapy at the graduate school of Nagoya University. Dr. Shibuya, one of the leading neurosurgeons with certification from the Japan Neurosurgical Society, worked in the Neurosurgery Department of Nagoya and Tokai Universities.

In 1997, he wrote a book titled *Subeteno Inochie: Something Great Karano Okurimono* (To all lives: A gift from something great) (Sougohourei Pubishing). In this book, he introduced sound-energy therapy as a method to cure various diseases by using the hado of voice. For complete details, please refer to Dr. Shibuya's book. Basically, he explains the therapy to find an individual's hado through his or her voice and to have him/her listen to the sound that corrects the disturbances.

The system for this therapy was developed by a Canadian engineer named Robert Roy. For thirty-five years, he devoted himself to studying this subject. He had a mathematician develop a mathematical formula to compute atomic frequencies. By using this formula, a sound is found to correct the disturbed frequency.

In early 2003, Mr. Roy further improved the system and developed software capable of creating a suitable sound after having a person vocalize for fifteen seconds. (Unlike a piece of music that has a melody, this system uses a single sound in various patterns.) This software makes it possible to create sounds much more easily than with the old version. It takes about three minutes to complete. (See figure 4.7.)

I tried it myself. As I was exhausted after an overseas travel and I was also quite busy writing, I had very stiff shoulders with some pain. After listening to the sound created by the software for thirty minutes, the stiffness in my shoulders suddenly disappeared.

If this new system becomes popular, music therapy would be able to make a quantum leap, because the sound with the most suitable information can be delivered to our individual cells. At my company, we are studying this sound-energy system.

Tune in to the Wavelength of Health and Happiness

When I wake up in the morning, I sit up and settle down. Then I gaze at the glass of water pre-placed at my bedside.

For about thirty seconds, I verbalize my gratitude by saying things like "I thank you, and I ask you for a nice day today." Then I drink half of the water. Next I think about what I need to do during the day. With the feeling of success that I imagine upon completing each task, I say to the water, "Everything went well, and I thank you." Then I drink the remaining water.

By doing so, the good information is sent not only to the water in the glass but also to the moisture in the surrounding air. It is possible to resonate with both the water in the glass and the moisture in the air.

I get up and go to the bathroom. After relieving myself, I say "thank you" to the flushing water with my feeling of gratitude.

I then take a shower. The shower water includes chlorine, and it is not good for the skin. Love and gratitude is necessary to improve its hado. This is especially important for those who have skin problems and may not be able to install a shower filter. It is a good idea to tape words such as "thank you" and "love and gratitude" on the wall of the shower room to improve the hado of the water.

When I have some time in the morning, I try to go for a walk. Basking in the morning sun brightens my heart. While I walk leisurely, I think of positive things.

Some people might think, "I cannot spare any time in the morning." If you want, you can create your time in the morning. All you have to do is to get up earlier. To get up early, you need to go to bed early. Too much drinking of alcohol has to be avoided. Just by spending your time in the morning leisurely, you can expect to live a well-regulated life that is good for you.

A breakfast follows. Usually, I have my breakfast with my wife; but even if I am by myself, I always say grace: "Itadakimasu" (Let me enjoy this meal).

As mentioned in the beginning of this chapter, it is better to use a variety of ingredients for cooking. Responding to this desire of mine, my wife puts her time and labor into cooking. I am full of gratitude for her.

While I eat, I am careful to chew my food well. By doing so, I am taking my time for eating. Gobbling does not make me enjoy the rich experience of eating my food. Taking time to enjoy eating has a calming effect on me.

After I finish eating, I drink tea unhurriedly. A saying goes, "A tea stem in your cup in the morning will bring luck to you." I interpret this as, "Have your breakfast with time to spare so that you will be able to notice a tea stem in your cup." If there is indeed a tea stem in my cup, I will be grateful and will feel more positive about the day. This positive attitude will lead me to the day's positive outcomes.

At the end of my breakfast, I say, "I have enjoyed my meal very much," or "Thank you very much," even if I am by myself.

Since I need to know what is going on in society, I usually watch the morning news and talk show on television. However, if they are going to focus on negative topics, I change the channel. In terms of hado, it would be healthier to watch major-league baseball than programs in distress. Watching sport games gives us good information, because while we watch a sports game, we are moved by a play from time to time. The deep impression of this has the effect of good hado and resonates with your body.

Then I go to work. During my commute, I also make myself think positively. I imagine how I will be successful at what I will be doing during the day. I call up the image of the guest coming to see me and the image of conversing nicely. Or I may come to think, "Well, my employees are working very hard. I should have a 'thank you' event for them. What about a group trip to Hawaii with all employees, say in February of next year?" Then I imagine that trip. The image of my employees, who work so hard, smiling and enjoying the island of everlasting summer brings me more willingness to do it.

I arrive at my office. I see my guest and start our conversation. Many ideas may pop up during our chatting. Some of the visitors look around my office carefully and ask, "In terms of hado, is there a good layout for an office or a home? How about furniture? Is a certain kind of furniture good or bad for generating hado?" This is the realm of Feng Shui experts. I don't have such knowledge; I have no advice to give in this regard. However, there is one thing I want to add from the viewpoint of hado.

It is better to open the windows as often as you can to exchange air. When water stagnates, its quality deteriorates. When it flows in a river, water does not get dirty. However, when water comes to a lake or a pond, it gets stale quickly. The same is true with the moisture in the air. So I am mindful about creating a flow of the air.

After work, I sometimes feel like drinking, so I often take my employees out. I make sure that such an occasion will be a free and easy party and that they will feel comfortable speaking freely even to their president.

The greatest merit of drinking is that people become freer to speak from their true feelings. We can strip off our armor. Through our heart-to-heart conversations, I am often impressed unexpectedly to find what they are thinking. These kinds of deep impressions generate good hado and seep into our cells.

In my company, no negative topic is allowed at the party. We often see a group of workers get together to drink and talk ill of their bosses. That kind of drinking party is not good. These people seem to be attracted to each other and enjoy resonating with their negative vibrations.

Interestingly, the places where these people go seem to attract similar parties of negative nature. Perhaps each group's vibration is resonating with one another. Such places are full of hado that I don't want to absorb. In this sense, it is important to carefully choose where you go to have parties.

I believe the intrinsic hado of alcohol is good. It merges with both water and oil. It is a rare substance that can bridge between water, spirituality, and materialism. Alcohol is considered to have a hado that we humans need. Of course, it is not good to drink alcohol to the extent that you cannot get up the next morning, so limit your drinking to a moderate amount.

I drink water before I go to bed. In a manner similar to my morning ritual, I talk to water for about three minutes in gratitude for the day.

I can clearly say that my day begins with water and ends with water. I am water, so I feel it to be very natural.

CHAPTER FIVE

As We Live,
Let's Dialogue with Water

It All Depends on Your Mental Attitude

Dr. Joan Davis is one of the readers who felt moved by reading about hado and viewing the pictures of water crystals in my books. Dr. Davis is a retired professor at Zurich Technical University, and she has researched water for over thirty years.

Dr. Davis said this to me:

Your research into taking water ice-crystal pictures suggests to us two very important points:

One is to become aware that water responds to even delicate energy. I also want to let scientists and officials know that there is almost no protection currently being provided for water. I feel this technique can be used in the fields of health and medical care.

Another is to give more respect to water. The important thing is that we recover our desire to treat water with respect.

In ancient Greece, people paid true respect for water, and many Greek myths are based on the protection of water. But then science appeared and rejected these myths because they were not scientific. Water lost its mystique and became just another substance.

In our modern culture, we have lost our attitude of respect for water and have been heading in the direction that technology could clean up as necessary. We sometimes say "Purified water is not pure." Water processed in treatment plants is not the water that forms beautiful crystals. What water requires is not purification but respect.

I was deeply moved by her saying, "Give respect to water." These are the words from a scientist who has worked in Switzerland, the advanced nation in water research.

Prayers Change Water

Pure water differs from technologically purified water. Dr. Davis's statement to this effect reminded me of an experiment we did some time ago.

We decided to conduct a grand experiment according to what Dr. Nobuo Shioya asserted about the spirit of words. Before World War II, Dr. Shioya was an assistant professor who taught at Keijyo Imperial University, Department of Medicine, in Seoul, Korea. Upon his return to Japan, he opened a clinic of internal medicine. He researched Seimeisen Chiryo (Lifeline therapy) and used it in his practice. At the age of more than one hundred years, he is still so fit that he enjoys playing golf every day. Dr. Shioya encourages us to say his prayer, which he calls the "Great Declaration": "The infinite power of the universe congeals and congeals; the world became truly great and peaceful." The point is to say it positively in the past tense, that is, "became." I have been influenced by it.

Well then, what was our experiment?

At 4:30 A.M. on July 25, 1999, as many as 350 people gathered together near Lake Biwa, the largest lake in Japan. Tradition says, "When Lake Biwa's water gets clear, the whole nation's water gets clear."

Lake Biwa had been polluted. Its dirty water smelled bad, and its beautiful colony of reeds had disappeared. In summer, a non-native algae from

Canada would grow abnormally and give off a foul smell, which had become a public concern in the area.

It was regrettable. Lake Biwa is Japan's mother lake. If the amniotic fluid of the mother's womb was polluted, what kind of negative influences would it have on the whole nation?

So we decided to rise up to purify the water of Lake Biwa with the power of hado. In the early, refreshing morning of the summer, Dr. Shioya led us in reciting the Great Declaration ten times.

One month later, on August 27, the Kyoto newspaper had a big article with the heading, "No abnormal growth of non-native algae this summer, zero odor." The article included this paragraph:

However, there are hardly any colonies covering the surface of the lake this year, and there is no complaint about odor due to the small Canadian algae. The amount of algae reaped this time last year reached about 1,500 tons, but this year, including the other kinds of algae, it remains at about 110 tons. The person in charge of the section [the prefecture's eco-life promotion section] commented, "I can't think of any case where the amount was so low. We are planning to ask experts' opinions and look into the causes."

It is natural to assume that the cause, which the prefecture's government wanted to know, was the hado of the Great Declaration. What do you think? (See figure 5.1.)

While I was convinced that the power of hado could change the largest lake in Japan, a heading in the newspaper *Sankei* on April 16 of the following year caught my eye: "Ultrasound decomposes dioxin in water: Useful for purification of lakes and marshes." This article introduced the research results of Professor Yasuaki Maeda, Osaka Prefecture University, College of Engineering. It left a great impact on me, as I had been looking for scientific evidence for my idea.

The organic substances such as dioxin and PCB (polychlorinated biphenyl) in water decomposed almost completely by using ultrasound waves; it was revealed on the 15th that the technology was developed by Professor Yasuaki Maeda, Osaka Prefecture University, College of Engineering. Passing the ultrasound waves of 200 kilohertz through water creates very tiny bubbles that absorb chemical compounds. When the bubbles burst, the chemical compounds are decomposed. It can be used for the purification of the contaminated water in lakes and marshes as well as for decomposing fluorocarbon, which destroys the ozone layer of the atmosphere. These substances are characterized as difficult to decompose; therefore, it has been a problem to be solved. When this technology is made fit for practical use, it will create a sensation both at home and abroad.

Ultrasound waves are the sounds higher than the range of audible sounds for humans (16,000 to 20,000 hertz). Due to the pressurization and depressurization under water, the waves generate the bubbles in the sizes of microns. A bubble is short-lived; it takes only 0.1 microsecond (1/100,000 second) to burst. The recent study shows that when a bubble gives in and bursts due to the water pressure around it, the bubble temporarily generates the heat of more than 5,000°C and the pressure of about 1,000 atmospheres.

As the organic chlorinated compounds have poor affinity with water, they stick to the bubbles. Due to the heat and pressure of the bursting bubbles, the compounds are decomposed to harmless carbonic acid gas and chloride ions. In the experiment, by passing the 200 kilohertz ultrasound through the PCB solution of 10 PPM for thirty minutes, 95 percent of the PCB was decomposed, and similar results were obtained with dioxin and fluorocarbon. As a way to remove chemical compounds from water, this method of de-chlorinating the compounds by irradiating ozone and ultraviolet rays is now close to practical use. The method of using 200 kilohertz ultrasound, which is harmless to the human body, is said to treat water safely and inexpensively.

At the time of this article about how water resonated with the vibrations of ultrasound waves that improved its quality, the sounds of the Great Declaration were echoing throughout the area at Lake Biwa.

I believe that these words are based on the sounds of Nature and were developed by learning from Nature. So when we said the word "universe," it had the same hado as the universe; thus, I believe it must have reached the universe. The Great Declaration states, "The infinite power of the universe..." The pure hado of our prayer must have traveled the ultrasound zone far away in the universe, resonated with it, and came back to the lake.

This event had a sequel.

My concept of hado tends to be not well accepted and understood by many who think that modern science is a panacea. I have been thinking that if I could work with the people on the side of modern science and have an information exchange on each other's results, we would be able to send our messages on hado widely to the general public.

The hado that I had been talking about and the new technology of Professor Maeda turned out to be covered together in an article. It appeared in the newspaper *Sankei* on March 13, 2003, in the sixth of a series of articles titled "Water science." Under the subheading, "Responding to ultrasound, harmful substances decompose," the results of Professor Maeda's research were reported again. Additionally, the research about playing music to water, which I had been doing, was introduced.

In the future, I believe that the energy of hado will attract more and more attention widely and open-heartedly. This will be wonderful.

My research shows that hado changes water. If we dialogue with water with a positive attitude and with respect, water will definitely change. Even the water in a big lake can change. The water in your body can also change.

"Let's Do It!" Rather Than "Do It!"

One of the people who became interested in our water-crystal pictures is a charming Swiss lady named

Manuela Kihm. Ms. Kihm, who runs an event-production company, appreciated the pictures of my book from early on. She said, "The wonder of water-crystal photographs is that we can see them with our own eyes. As a result, our consciousness makes a rapid leap. This awakening of the consciousness happens very quickly. The fact that things that we have thought and felt can be seen with our eyes accelerates this change." Consequently, she invited me to give a lecture in Switzerland. The success at that time led me to visit Europe every year for lectures.

Ms. Kihm continued to say, "As I have two children, I know that whether I talk to them lovingly or just give them an order makes a big difference on them. It is different to say 'Let's do it!' or 'Do it!' Also, I do understand that we feel it at the level of each cell in the body."

The expressions "Let's do it!" and "Do it!" are both frequently used by parents when they discipline their children. The children who hear these expressions would feel differently depending on the expression used. If you were a child, how would you like to be talked to?

We pasted labels with the words "Let's do it!" and "Do it!" on two bottles of water and took photographs. (See figure 5.2.)

As predicted, the water labeled "Let's do it!" formed a crystal. It has a shape apt to be called cute rather than beautiful. On the other hand, the water shown "Do it!" made only the shape of frightening circle. After all, demands and orders do not carry good hado.

"Love" and "Gratitude" Change the World

Water responded to words used for talking to children. This made me think that water might respond to information regarding mothers and fathers who pour love on their offspring. After writing various words on paper, we showed them to water.

For information regarding mothers, I selected "the taste of mother's cooking," "mother's care," "wife and mother-in-law," "umbilical cord," "happy home," "childbirth," "mother's milk," "child care," and "sense of security." Except for one, all of them resulted in marvelous crystals. The one that did not form a complete crystal was "wife and mother-in-law." This phrase seems to include some negative information.

For information regarding fathers, I selected "father's hobby," "playing catch with father," "family trip," "father's teaching," "father's example," and "central pillar" (breadwinner). All of them formed crystals as we expected. (For full details, please see *Messages from Water*, Vol. 2.)

Somewhat contrary to my expectation was the water shown the Japanese word "central pillar."

I thought the water would form a big and strong shape of crystal. However, the actual crystal was compact and tiny. If the word "central pillar" had been shown to water when fathers were still thought of as the head of a family, the water might have formed a different crystal. The crystal we obtained may be a reflection of the reality of today's fathers who feel a little bit less respected. (See figure 5.3.)

In any event, water responded sensitively to the information regarding "love" and "gratitude" of a family.

Water was affected by the vibration with the feeling of "love" and "gratitude." This must be true with you who are water and the world you are in.

Ms. Kazue Kato was known as an activist of women's liberation and a politician in Japan. She won office in the first election after World War II and became the first woman member of the National Diet in Japan. Ms. Kato continued to offer new suggestions and contributed greatly to the enhancement of women's social status in Japan. She lived to be 104 years old. In an interview on her hundredth birthday, I recall, she was asked, "What is your secret for longevity?" She answered, "I have ten experiences a day that touch my heart. That is my secret for longevity."

I thought this was wonderful. I can understand what she meant very well. By having experiences that touch our heart, we can resonate with good hado, which in turn will correct any disturbances in our body's intrinsic hado.

In the morning, I get up and go out to see the sun. My heart is touched by the beauty of the bright sun, and I feel grateful that I am alive. I feel like worshiping the sun. Looking at the garden, I find beautiful morning-glory flowers that also touch my heart.

In this manner, if I can start my day with experiences that touch my heart, the day will turn out to be great.

If I were to describe the experience of being touched in exaggerated terms, it is to have an exchange of our vital forces. We resonate with each other. I receive the vibration from the sun and also from the morning-glory flowers. In return, I send my vibration to the sun and to the morning-glory flowers. When we can exchange wonderful vibrations, we can say that we are sharing our lives.

If you don't notice the brightly shining sun and the blooming morning-glory flowers, perhaps you are not ready to resonate with their wonderful vibrations. If your intrinsic vibration is such, your health may also be compromised.

No vibration means death. When we encounter something wonderful, let's feel our heart being touched; thus, let's resonate with fresh vibrations.

We must pay respect to water, feel love and grati-
tude, and receive vibrations with a positive attitude.
Then, water changes, you change, and I change.
Because both you and I are water.

Figure 4.2
What happens to water exposed to a cellular phone, a television set, and a personal computer?

Water having received electromagnetic waves from a cellular phone

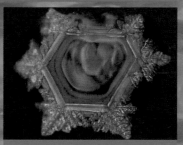

Water labeled "love and gratitude" having received electromagnetic waves from a cellular phone

We put distilled water into a bottle and tied a cellular phone on it with a string. We called the phone ten times and kept the line on in silence for a minute each time. The result was the picture above; however, the one with the label "love and gratitude" formed a crystal.

Figure 4.2 (*continued*)

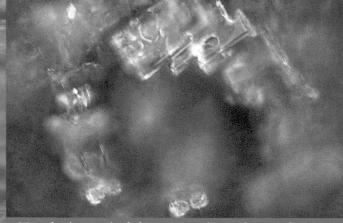

Water having received electromagnetic rays from a television set for four hours

Water labeled "love and gratitude" having received electromagnetic rays from a television set

The picture above was taken after having left a bottle of water in front of a television set for four hours. Looking at it seems to make our eyes tired. On the other hand, the water labeled "love and gratitude" was able to form a hexagonal crystal nicely.

Figure 4.2 (*continued*)

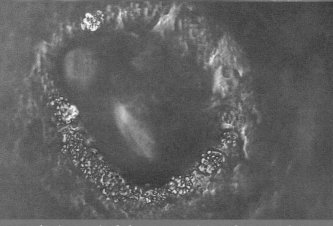

Water having received electromagnetic rays from a PC for
four hours

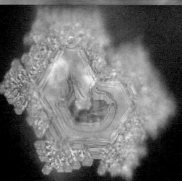

Water labeled "love and gratitude"
having received electro-magnetic
rays from a PC

After having left a bottle of water in front of a personal computer
for four hours, the distilled water in the bottle with no label showed a
terrifying circular shape. On the other hand, the one labeled "love and
gratitude" exposed to the electromagnetic waves of a PC was shining as
shown on the right.

Figure 4.3
A good television program can also heal water

Water shown a public-television documentary program
A videotape titled Life was shown to water. Depending on the television
program, water can form a beautiful crystal even without the label of
"love and gratitude."

Figure 4.4
Playing music to a bottle of water placed between two speakers

Figure 4.5
Good music pleases and heals water

"Canon in D Major," Pachelbel

Water responded to beautiful pieces of music by forming elegant crystals, while it clearly reacted negatively to heavy-metal music. This doesn't necessarily mean that heavy-metal music is bad, but the lyrics of this piece seemed to be problematic.

Figure 4.5 (*continued*)

"Time to Say Goodbye," Sarah Brightman and Andrea Bocelli

A piece of heavy-metal music

Figure 4.6
Our body, mind, and water respond to good music

"Canon in D Major," Pachelbel
Emotional hado: Relief from anxiety and uneasiness
Physical hado: Uterus, ovaries

The water crystal after listening to this canon revealed a unique shape. Like the motif of this piece, the crystal had layers. As for the body's parts, the music resonated with the uterus and ovaries. As a matter of fact, my wife likes this piece very much, and she listened to it often when she was pregnant. It would be good for prenatal care of an unborn child. The influence of anxiety and uneasiness on a fetus shouldn't be made light of.

Figure 4.6 (*continued*)

"Toccata and Fugue in D Minor," Bach
Emotional hado: Relief from lethargy
Physical hado: Right cerebrum

This crystal has an unspoiled look. It reminded us of the deep sound of a pipe organ and seemed to be stretching upward to the heavens. When this picture's hado was measured, it resulted in vitalizing the right brain and canceling the hado of lethargy. This solemn piece of Bach's music certainly has the motivational feel of vibration for the listeners. Dr. Schweitzer is known for his dedicated medical activities and for being a talented organist. This piece is said to be one of his favorites. Perhaps the toccata and fugue was a driving force for his activities.

Figure 4.6 (*continued*)

"March No.1," Elgar
Emotional hado: Relief from shyness and bashfulness
Physical hado: Spine, spinal cord
The water crystal after listening to Elgar's "March No.1" had a sturdy, dignified, and stable shape. The hado measurements of this photograph are given above. Without courage and confidence, we cannot march in a dignified way. This march causes us to naturally straighten our spine. This piece is recommended for those who don't feel confident speaking in front of people.

Figure 4.6 (*continued*)

"Time to Say Goodbye," Sarah Brightman and Andrea Bocelli
Emotional hado: Relief from passiveness and negativity
Physical hado: Colon, rectum

This piece was a big hit in the world and became very popular in Japan, as it was used in a commercial. This piece has a seemingly sad title, but the result of the hado measurements made me think that the "goodbye" in this song must be a positive one. I found that the meaning of the song was to depart together with the loved one. Departure comes with farewell, but when we can take it positively, we may be able to solve a problem on which we've been "stuck."

Figure 4.6 (*continued*)

Prelude from *Carmen*, Bizet
Emotional hado: Relief from suppression
Physical hado: Circulatory system

Just like Carmen, heroine of the opera, this crystal appeared to be free and uninhibited. Contrary to its tragic ending, this piece has an uplifting effect on the listener. From my experience, a crystal like this one is only possible when the piece of music is exquisite and precise. The results of our hado measurements are given above. The way Carmen lives, she doesn't suppress anything. Carmen depicts a woman who dances the flamenco in passionate rhythm and lives her life as she desires.

Figure 4.6 (*continued*)

The Moldau, Smetana
Emotional hado: Relief from irritability
Physical hado: Lymph
The water-crystal photograph after having played The Moldau resulted in the hado measurement of canceling the hado of irritability. In terms of physical hado, it resonated strongly with the lymphatic system. By listening to this piece, we can expect to relieve the hado of irritability and vitalize the lymphatic system. When you feel irritable, it is a sign that inside you are telling yourself that you need calmness and freedom from pressure. By being kinder to yourself, your mind will become clearer.

Figure 4.6 (*continued*)

"The Blue Danube," Johann Strauss Jr.
Emotional hado: Relief from lost vigor due to prolonged endurance
Physical hado: Central nervous system

By listening to "The Blue Danube" waltz, the central nervous system organs that had been withered due to habitual endurance will be vitalized. You will be able to feel relaxed and big-hearted at both body and mind levels. To you who are sincere and serious with your acquired habit of endurance since your childhood, your cells are saying, "You don't have to endure anymore. Let's live freely."

Figure 4.6 (*continued*)

"Danube Waves," Joseph Ivanovitch
Emotional hado: Relief from suppression
Physical hado: Promotion of blood circulation
Listening to "Danube Waves" will help you to express your feelings without suppressing them. When your heart opens to your true feelings, the stagnant blood circulation will be smoother; thus, the cells must be more activated. Besides suppression, the other hado of emotions that stagnates the bodily fluid (blood) are stubbornness, greediness, and excess fear.

Figure 4.6 (*continued*)

Swan Lake, Act 2, Tchaikovsky
Emotional hado: Obsession
Physical hado: Joints

Like a swan dances in the lake, let's remove our guard (fixed ideas) that we have built inside us and behave freely. While listening to *Swan Lake*, you might want to move your body a little more freely. Together with bodily joints, your thoughts will become more flexible.

Figure 4.7
A sound-energy system

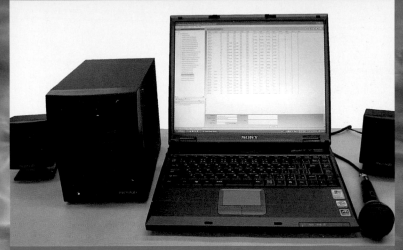

Through a microphone, the voice is recorded. Then a computer creates a sound that will correct the person's disturbed hado.

Figure 5.1
Gratitude and prayers purify Lake Biwa

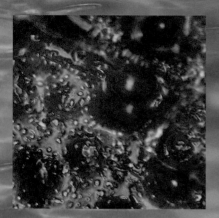

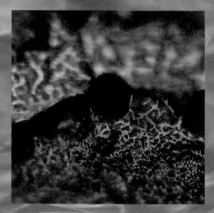

Water before the experiment
These pictures show the water of Lake Biwa before we conducted our prayer experiment in July 1999. As the photographs were terrible, we doubted if we were really seeing our mother lake, and it made us feel like looking away.

Figure 5.1 (*continued*)

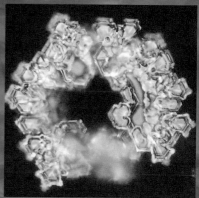

Water after the experiment

Water six months later

After the experiment, we sampled the water and photographed ice crystals. These seemed to indicate the process of water purification. During the summer of 1999, Lake Biwa did not have any offensive odor. The water sampled in January 2000, six months after the prayer, formed a more orderly crystal.

Figure 5.2
The power of words that water teaches us

Let's do it!

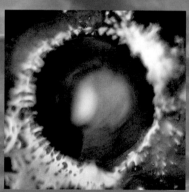

Do it!

Perhaps an imperative form is not part of Nature's providence.
"Let's do it!" resulted in a free and easy cute crystal, while "Do
it!" created only the circle at the bottom. Which expression
would you choose?

Figure 5.3
How water responds to words about mothers and fathers

Taste of mother's cooking

Instant food

Although "taste of mother's cooking" is different for different people, all of the crystals we photographed from the water in fifty petri dishes were orderly and beautiful. Perhaps it is because everyone has "taste of mother's cooking" as his or her tender and beautiful memory. On the other hand, instant food's crystal was not so beautiful.

Figure 5.3 (*continued*)

Mother's care

Daughter-in-law and
mother-in-law

The photographs on this page are in monochrome, but the actual color of the crystal with "mother's care" was slightly pinkish. According to a specialist, pink has the power of caring, love, and activating vital force. The kanji character for "daughter-in-law" writes a woman being at home and that for "mother-in-law" an old woman. Is that why they are often not so friendly?

Figure 5.3 (*continued*)

Family trip

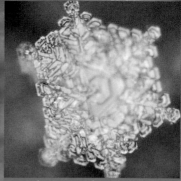
Playing catch with father

The breadwinner

Rather than saying you're too busy and tired, setting aside family time on weekends is important. Otherwise, I am a bit afraid that the presence of "the breadwinner" may get even smaller than this one when we next take another picture of water crystals exposed to this word.

The Hidden Messages in Water
$16.95, softcover

New York Times best-selling author Masaru Emoto shares the realizations he has gained by combining the latest scientific research with the knowledge he has drawn from his years of studying water in *The Hidden Messages in Water*. Emoto's main objective and passion is the healing of water, mankind, and the earth. By expressing love to water, one can create a small, beautiful universe. Our consciousness, eyes, and mind, when full of goodwill, breathe new life into water and help us heal by using the most simple resource: water. His research has visually captured the structure of water at the moment of freezing, and through high-speed photography Emoto has shown the direct consequences of destructive thoughts or, alternatively, the thoughts of love and appreciation on the formation of water crystals. Filled with 64 pages of full-color photographs, and over 100 photographs in total, *The Hidden Messages in Water* provides empowering proof that water is alive and responsive to our every emotion.

To order, contact

Beyond Words Publishing, Inc.
20827 N.W. Cornell Road, Suite 500, Hillsboro, OR 97124-9808
503-531-8700

You can also visit our Web site at *www.beyondword.com*
or e-mail us at *info@beyondword.com*.

**Masaru Emoto's self-published books,
Messages from Water, Volumes 1, 2, and 3 are
available in English with Japanese subtitles.**

Messages from Water, Vol. 1, ISBN: 4-939098-00-1
$32.00, hardcover
This book outlines the beginning of Masaru Emoto's
work, how he came upon his idea for photographing
water crystals, how the environment influences
water, and problems with contamination and quality.

Messages from Water, Vol. 2, ISBN: 4-939098-004-4
$39.95, softcover
This volume shows how water is negatively affected
by the electromagnetic waves from computers, TVs,
and cell phones. Also included in this second book
is a section comparing crystals of the same word in
different languages.

Messages from Water, Vol.3, ISBN: 4-939098-05-2
$39.95, softcover
Ten years after publishing his first volume, Masaru
Emoto has published a book around the theme of
prayer, especially regarding world peace, beginning
with each person learning to love himself or herself.

**Additional products inspired by Masaru Emoto available
from Beyond Words Publishing**

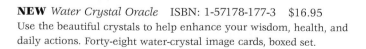

NEW *Water Crystal Oracle*   ISBN: 1-57178-177-3 $16.95
Use the beautiful crystals to help enhance your wisdom, health, and
daily actions. Forty-eight water-crystal image cards, boxed set.

"Words Purify Water" Water Bottles

One-liter durable plastic water bottles. Available in 3 colors: ice blue, royal blue, and emerald green.
$10.00 each

Water-Crystal Coasters

Fill your water glass with Love & Thanks as it rests on the water-crystal coaster.
$10.00 each

Water-Crystal Stickers

Twenty-eight water-crystal stickers to change the atmosphere of whatever you place them on in a positive way, such as "The God of Wealth" for your wallet or "Love & Thanks" for your cell phone.
$10.00 per sheet

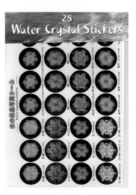

Hidden Messages in Water
Portland, Oregon, lecture DVD

Masaru Emoto speaks about his water research. Learn how you can affect water with your thoughts and words and what you can do to preserve this precious resource. In Japanese with simultaneous English translation. Recorded April 2004.

Approximately 2 hours.
ISBN: 1-58270-125-3
$20.00

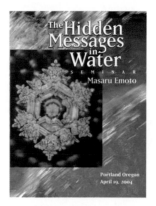

Messages from Water
DVD or Video

• Observations and experiments
• Exposing words and music to water
• Interview with Masaru Emoto and more . . .

Approximately 45 minutes.
ISBN: 09665312-4-8
$20.00

Healing Music CDs from Beyond Words Publishing, Inc.

Alan Roubik is recognized as Japan's top "Healing Music" artist and producer. Tested and endorsed by Masaru Emoto, who has said that Alan's music has the most healing properties of any modern music. His recordings are used for pain and anxiety relief and for assisting the human immune system.

CD2000: MUSIC FOR YOUR HEALTH

CD2000 was created using unique mathematical formulas and theories for the purpose of easing pain, enhancing physical immunity, and assisting in the relief of stress and anxiety. Each song was tested for water crystal formation by Masaru Emoto and this recording has been recommended by doctors worldwide. Featured in Masaru Emoto's books.

One CD, $20.00

KEYS TO MY HEART

Keys To My Heart is a Solo piano recording of original compositions that are great for relaxation, massage, romantic encounters, stress relief, and more. Results indicate that various vital organs are affected by the resonance of each composition. Featured in *Water Crystal Oracle* and *Messages from Water*, Volume 2.

One CD, $20.00

THE FOUR SEASONS

A musical blend of new age, modern jazz, and classical influences, this recording was the first of its kind, proven in a laboratory that music can indeed be created specifically for therapeutic application. Featured in *Messages from Water*, Volume 1.
One CD, $20.00

SEVEN CHAKRAS & ELEMENTS

The word chakra is Sanskrit for wheel or disk and signifies one of seven basic energy centers in the body. Authentic and sacred instruments from Tibet, China, South America and Africa were used in the recording of this CD which features songs created with very specific chakra guidelines, including frequency, key, and Hz.
Two-CD set, $30.00

WATER SONG

With original lyrics written by Masaru Emoto, *Water Song* features the music of composer and musician Aman Ryusuke Seto. The songs on the CD were created to encourage respect and love for water throughout the world and the lyrics and melodies are truly beautiful and inspiring.
One CD, $24.95

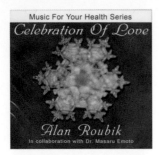

Music For Your Health Series
Celebration Of Love
Alan Roubik
In collaboration with Dr. Masaru Emoto

CELEBRATION OF LOVE

The *Celebration of Love* two-CD set includes instrumental and solo piano versions of original contemporary music composed by Alan Roubik, as well as original arrangements of music composed by Mendelssohn, Schubert, Gruber, Handel, and Joplin. The instrumental CD primarily features piano, guitar, bass, flute, oboe, saxophone, duduk, and percussion. Two-CD set, $30.00

Other Books from Beyond Words Publishing, Inc.

The Power of Appreciation
The Key to a Vibrant Life
Authors: Noelle C. Nelson, Ph.D.,
and Jeannine Lemare Calaba, Psy.D.
$14.95, softcover

Research confirms that when people feel appreciation, good things happen to their minds, hearts, and bodies. But appreciation is much more than a feel-good mantra. It is an actual force, an energy that can be harnessed and used to transform our daily life—relationships, work, health and aging, finances, crises, and more.

The Art of Thank You
Crafting Notes of Gratitude
Author: Connie Leas
$14.95, hardcover

While reminding us that a little gratitude can go a long way, this book distills the how-tos of thank-yous. Part inspirational, part how-to, *The Art of Thank You* will rekindle the gratitude in all of us and inspire readers to pick up a pen and take the time to show thanks. It stresses the healing power that comes from both giving and receiving thanks and provides practical, concrete, and inspirational examples.

Forgiveness
The Greatest Healer of All
Author: Gerald G. Jampolsky, M.D.
Foreword: Neale Donald Walsch
$12.95, softcover

Forgiveness: The Greatest Healer of All is written in simple, down-to-earth language. It explains why so many of us find it difficult to forgive and why holding on to grievances is really a decision to suffer. The book describes what causes us to be unforgiving and how our minds work to justify this. It goes on to point out the toxic side effects of being unforgiving and the havoc it can play on our bodies and on our lives. But above all, it leads us to the vast benefits of forgiving.

A B O U T   T H E   A U T H O R

Masaru Emoto was born in Yokohama in July 1943. He is a graduate of the Yokohama Municipal University's department of humanities and sciences, with a focus on International Relations. In 1986 he established the IHM Corporation in Tokyo. In October of 1992 he received certification from the Open International University as a Doctor of Alternative Medicine. Subsequently he was introduced to the concept of micro-cluster water in the United States, and Magnetic Resonance Analysis technology. The quest thus began to discover the mystery of water.

Masaru Emoto undertook extensive research into water around the planet, not so much as a scientific researcher but more from the perspective of an original thinker. At length he realized that it was in the frozen crystal form that water showed us its true nature. He continues with this experimentation and has written a variety of well-received books in Japanese, as well as the seminal *Messages from Water*, published bilingually. He is married to Kazuko Emoto, who shares his passion and is head of Kyoikusha, the publishing arm of his company. They have three children.

Beyond Words Publishing, Inc.

OUR CORPORATE MISSION
Inspire to Integrity

OUR DECLARED VALUES
We give to all of life as life has given us.
We honor all relationships.
Trust and stewardship are integral to fulfilling dreams.
Collaboration is essential to create miracles.
Creativity and aesthetics nourish the soul.
Unlimited thinking is fundamental.
Living your passion is vital.
Joy and humor open our hearts to growth.
It is important to remind ourselves of love.

To order contact

Beyond Words Publishing, Inc.
20827 N.W. Cornell Road, Suite 500
Hillsboro, OR 97124-9808
503-531-8700

You can also visit our Web site at *www.beyondword.com*
or e-mail us at *info@beyondword.com*.